Finding Your
Inner Gift

Finding Your Inner Gift

The Ultimate
Reiki First Degree Manual

Marnie Vincolisi

This book is not intended as a substitute for the medical recommendations of physicians or other health-care providers. Rather,
it is intended to offer alternative information to help the reader cooperate with physicians and health professionals in a mutual quest for optimal well-being and a better understanding of self.

Published by Light Internal
Littleton, Colorado
www.lightinternal.com

Book covers design by Rich Allen
Photograph of author by Eric Weber

ISBN 978-0-9823732-0-0

Price $13.95

Dedication

It is with love and respect I dedicate this book to my students and clients who have graced my life over the years. It is through their eyes I have been gifted the knowledge found within the pages of this book.

The Greatest good you can do for another
is not just to share your riches,
but to reveal to him his own.

Benjamin Disraeli

My wish is to reveal to you the power and abilities
which are yours and yours alone.

Marnie Vincolisi

Table of Contents

Introduction 1

Chapter 1 11

The Gift of Reiki 11

    Benefits of Reiki 21

    Origin of Reiki 24

       The Two Precepts of Reiki 28

       Traditional and Non-Traditional Reiki 31

       Traditional Reiki Masters 33

       Degrees of Reiki 34

Chapter 2 37

How Reiki Works 37

    Attunements 42

       The Attunement Process 44

       The 21-Day Cleanse Process 45

    The Process of Using Reiki 50

       Reiki I Guidelines 51

       Activating the Reiki Energy 52

       Balancing Chakras 52

       Procedures to Balance the Chakras 53

       Grounding 53

       Life Tool: Grounding Cosmic Energy 55

    Self-Treatment 57

       Self Healing Hand Positions 60

Chapter 3 67

The Symbols 67

    The Power Symbol 71

       How to Activate the Power Symbol 73

       How to Use the Power Symbol 74

Chapter 4 78

The Chakras 78

    Life Tool: Chakra Opening 85

       Qualities of Chakras 87

Chapter 5 90

The Treatment 90

    Preparation before Giving a Treatment 93

    Treatment with Hands off the Body 94

    Scanning 96

How to Scan 97

Self-Scanning 98

Beaming 98

Reiki Treatment for Others 100

Hand Positions for Others 101

Closing 103

After the Session 104

Hand Positons for Healing Others 105

Treatments for Children and Animals 112

Teenagers 113

Animals 113

Plants 114

Practical Hands-on Healing 115

Preparation of the Space before a Healing Treatment 117

Aura Energy Boost 118

Life Tool: Aura Energy Boost 120

Meditation 121

Life Tool: Golden Light Transfer 122

Life Tool: Chakra Meditation 123

Chapter 6 125

The Forms 125

Recipient Information Form 127

Progress and Treatment Report 128

What is a Reiki Treatment? 129

Chakra Cleansing Journal 131

Afterword 137

Notes 139

Appendix 142

Bibliography 144

Index 145

About the Author 145

Programs by Marnie Vincolisi 150

Introduction

Reiki healing is an inherent part of our physical being. It can lay dormant until it is awakened within us by an attunement process given by a Reiki master teacher, but in fact we have always possessed this healing light. In this society unfortunately many of our intuitive natural abilities are ignored and often invalidated. By living in this cloud of denial we can become confused and lose sight of who we really are. This can manifest in low self-esteem, anger, infidelity and lack of confidence or compassion for our fellow man and the earth. It all stems from lack of love. When we open to receive the gift of Reiki we open to reclaim our ability to love and be loved. There is nothing difficult about using this God given energy. The process is simple and yet in its simplicity it can appear complex.

I was guided by my spirit to write this book based on the fact that many Reiki practitioners have been attuned to Reiki but do not fully understand how to use this energy to fulfill and enhance their daily life. I also wanted to address the mass of mankind who have not, as of yet, discovered their inner gift and the ability to transform their lives into what their heart desires.

What makes me an expert in teaching and performing Reiki? Nothing. My gift is no greater than yours. The difference is I have discovered how to become aware of the unseen and listen to the many messages which are presented to us daily. I am not talking about voices in my head or messages from guides or words flashing before me. I am referring to paying attention to nature, animals, billboards, songs on the radio and sensing the world around me. Reiki gives you the ability to become aware of information which is presented to you almost every day, perceive situations in a new light, which eases judgment, misunderstandings or criticism sometimes related to challenging situations.

I have always had the gift to love mankind and all around me but I really did not understand how to use it. Growing up, my family was loving in their own way, but they, like so many others, had been so emotionally injured they did not understand how to give or receive love. Living in this situation I felt like I was the one who was strange. I did not act like them, I did not think like them, and I did not even look like them. I loved to laugh and did it often and I was usually told, "Don't be so silly." As a child this confused me but now I see I was just being a kid, whose job is to be goofy and bring lightness into the stressful world of the adults. I find the sound of a child laughing is the sweetest sound on earth. I really cannot exist without it.

I recall a time when my mother must have been under a tremendous amount of stress. It was a warm summer night in Chicago and I was out walking around the neighborhood with my friends. As we turned the corner near my house, I saw my mother, red eyed and frantic. Even though the sun had not yet set, she was fearful and thought for sure something had happened to me. I was probably gone no more than an hour or two. A thought came to me and I expressed to my mom, "When it is my time to go, I will be gone. Now is not my time." Even at thirteen I held an inner wisdom greater than the adults around me, I knew I was protected by love and no harm would come to me. This is knowledge I have held and explained to others during my life.

As a child of the 1950s and a teenager of the 1960s, I did all the things that the society of that time expected of me. I got married instead of living with a boy. I had children and I blindly obeyed my mother even as an adult. But in my 40's my life began to change almost overnight. The transformation began after I met my father, a man whose love, unbeknownst to me, was hidden from me. Earlier in my life I had no contact to my roots. Meeting my dad and his family solved the mystery of who I was. Once I met my dad my husband Frank said, "Now the pieces fit together." He shared that there always seemed to be parts of me that did not seem to fit my puzzle, now the picture was complete.

All my life I was pouring out love with very little in return and now I was finally on the receiving end of love. Here was a family who loved me from afar. I was shocked. They had always missed me and were sad when my mom divorced my dad and took us away. What was surprising was how the people in this family spoke about my mom. They never said a negative word about her, they would

just say, "Water over the dam," and go on to another subject. They taught me more about love the afternoon I met my dad than I had been taught my entire life. I lay in bed that night in a state of bliss and wonder. How could I be so lucky to receive all this love and to know that I was loved and was worthy of love. It has taken me years to fully integrate this concept into my life and I feel it is one we all struggle to attain during our lives.

That meeting with my father started me on a path of self-discovery; one which I am glad never ends. I began to realize I had been given a gift. I am now able to express metaphysical concepts to others and they understand what I am saying. This has allowed others to transform their lives rather quickly. I now want to connect and share this message with more than my select group of students. That is the purpose of this book. To enlighten and assist mankind to their highest potential in a way that is simple. This transformation does not have to be complex. This is why I am compelled to share the gift of Reiki, because it channels love without a need to understand it. I rarely see someone untouched by its light. I see hearts open as people become gentler with themselves, which allows them to be kinder to others.

Not long after I met my dad I realized I was no longer working in a job that served my highest purpose. For fifteen years I ran a successful toy manufacturing company. It was a cottage industry involving my entire family. It served a purpose for a time as I was able to stay home with my three children while I fulfilled my creative nature and had an income. As the children grew and became more independent I found my physical presence was not always required. This gave me more time to look at what was important to me. Life, (or shall I say spirit), was directing me but it took me some time to follow the guidance.

Ever since I was nineteen years old I have been an entrepreneur. I began as a hairdresser in the Chicago area where I loved how I could interact with my patrons. I was able to use my creativity and I now see how that was the beginning of my counseling career. Women would come to me not just for a fresh new physical look but to express troubles in their life. From the compassion and love I held for their situations they would look and feel better inside and out.

I worked on straight commission and it taught me that if I didn't work, I didn't get paid. What a wonderful lesson to learn at such a young age. This empowered me to know my actions were always reflected in the results they attained. From hairdressing, I became a real estate agent, which was a short-lived profession. I did not like the up and down of the market and the home interest rates were at an all time high of eighteen percent. I did not know it in the moment but life was heading me in a different direction.

I now had an opportunity to create a job that kept me home with my children and still afforded me the opportunity to use my creative skills. Sewing was one of my many passions along with crafts of any kind. I knitted, crocheted, did macramé, weaved baskets, caned chairs, you name it. If I could use my hands artistically, I was doing it. The thought crossed my mind that all these endeavors could create income, so I started the PeeWeeTeePee Company. I recall my oldest daughter Carmin saying, (she has always been the realistic one) "You can't name a company that!" I replied, "Who would forget a name like this!". And so PeeWeeTeePee was born. We created play tents and toys for girls and boys. A few years later I noticed how kids loved to dress up so I added WannaBe & Company to the business, a costume line of children's play clothes.

My business gave me great joy as I was involved in all aspects of this small company. I created and designed the products and had a staff of 30 who produced most of the products. It was a joy to see my little customers dance off in capes, crowns and fairy wings. They were delighted to be adorned with their newly created images and I was in my element. My life began to change when fifteen years later I began to sense this vocation was not serving me and it was time to move on. My resistance was great, after all, I was making a good income and I was having fun, why stop now? Yet, in my heart, I knew an upcoming change was inevitable.

My biggest fear was the unknown. It wasn't like I could go out and just get a job. I never really worked for a company, as I had always worked for myself. I felt I had no skills and did not know where to start. I now realize how crazy that

thought was. Of course I had skills - I had created and had run a company single-handedly. Because of my low self esteem I could not see my value.

Life does not come with instructions or a glossary so there was no reference point for me to access when I knew change was at hand. I just needed to trust life's messages and to go with the flow. It took about two years to fully move into a place where I could make a change. The message to move on to a new vocation at first came in a soft voice but that voice became louder as time went on. My messages do not come in voices or guides at my bedside, they come from my observations of inanimate things around me. This communication was coming from my van.

You see, my van was the place I spent much of my time. I traveled over 40,000 miles a year pulling a 12' trailer, going to art shows to sell my wares. Talk about stress! I'm not very big, only five foot two inches tall and looked pretty funny behind the wheel of a big van. I hardly peeked over the wheel but none-the-less, there I was. In the summer of 1995, I was on a sales tour, first to Chicago and then on to Texas. These were pre-Christmas art and craft shows and in the past, they had been quite profitable. But life had another idea in mind.

In the middle of Iowa, on a sunny August day, the wheel of my van began to make a strange noise, so I pulled over to a gas station to investigate. Unfortunately there was no mechanic on duty and I was told I would have to continue for nine more miles to the next exit. I nervously stepped back into my van, got back onto the interstate, hands sweating, heart beating fast and wheels grinding. I needed help. There was no one I could see on this physical plane so I felt I might as well call in the ones who never left my side. I called in all of my angels.

The minutes felt like hours and at last I was at the exit I needed. It was a small town, one gas station, one café (not a restaurant, a café), and one motel. I pulled into the service station and as the mechanic jacked my van onto the lift, the wheel fell off. He looked up at me with intensity and said, "Lady there was an angel holding this wheel on." "I know," I replied. "I put her there." The bearings were gone - toast.

My intuition told me to ask him to check the other axle. He felt it was not necessary because both bearings would not go out at the same time. The voice in my head would not be still, so I told him to check it anyway. That axle was in almost the same condition, just about ready to go. He appeared to be a gentle soul and I felt his compassion as he informed me the parts needed would have to be ordered and would not be in for two days and another day to do the repairs. There was nothing to do but wait it out and get to the show late.

Waiting was and still is not one of my strong points, but there was nothing else I could do. It was now quite apparent I was not going to be able to sell my merchandise that weekend. Here was the scenario: it was the fall, I sold toys, this was the big push for Christmas. If I missed these two shows I was going to lose a big piece of my income for the holiday season.

This incident was at the end of a trail of many unfortunate circumstances that had occurred during the previous year. During my fifteen years in this business, I traveled forty thousand miles each year across the country without car trouble. If my van needed repair, it let me know when I was comfortably in my home town. I never missed an art show because of bad weather, accidents or van problems, until this year.

Even though the entire year I had van troubles, my angelic protectors were always by my side. When I had a problem with my van while I was out of town, I would miraculously be situated near a gas station. In May, I was on a stretch of road in New Mexico where there were no towns for seventy miles. I stepped on the gas pedal and it dropped to the floor; there was no acceleration in the van. I could see the town just ahead and I was able to coast down the hill, into the town and stopped directly in front of the gas station.

In July in Missouri at one art show, my trailer had a flat tire, my battery went dead and I left my keys for my trailer back in Colorado. All was taken care of in

divine order. The battery went dead at night at the hotel where I could recharge it. My flat tire was discovered just before I left to go home and I got to the tire store on a Sunday just before they closed. Once again my angels were with me. Each time I had a problem with the van, I knew it was a message to dissolve my business but I was not listening. If I quit this business now, what would I do? I found it easier to ignore my guidance than to step up to the plate and venture on and create a new business.

The situation in Iowa finally opened me to a new perception. I was being guided, no coerced, to get out of this business, for the Universe had something else in mind for me. I realized at this point, there was nothing else to do but trust the voice which was directing me, and my decision was made. As I walked into what appeared to be the "Bates Motel," I sat down on the bed and I spoke out loud to the Universe. "OK, I am listening, I quit." At that moment I folded my business.

My van was repaired and I drove home to Colorado and cried as I drove across the state line. I was home, what a relief. I was so busy running from my guidance I did not realize the stress I was under. Once I recognized I no longer needed to drive across the county by myself I let go. My tears reflected the emotion of peace and relief. Now all that I needed to do was wait for the Universe to give me my next orders. After all, I was finally listening!

I assumed the answer would no doubt come quickly, at least within a month or two, or three or four. Well, how about nine months? Yes, it took nine months for the Universe to present to me my next step. I now see those nine months were the gestation period I was given to prepare for my next step, for it was a big one.

Much to my surprise the next rung on my ladder turned out to be Reiki. I had heard about Reiki five years prior but the concept was quite foreign to me and I never really saw myself as a healer. Somehow exploring the healing arts felt right to pursue this time. My faith was being tested, for the Reiki master teacher suggested for my training was in Germany. I had never been off the North

American continent nor had never spoken another language, so this took a lot of faith to use my savings and go to meet a strange woman in a far away land. I had been out of work for nine months and a trip to Europe seemed rather extravagant.

Victoria Lyndt was the master teacher who attuned me in Germany. She was trained by Mrs. Phyllis Furumoto, who is Mrs. Hawayo Takata's, (grand master of Reiki) granddaughter. This is my lineage but as a non-traditional master I do not usually mention my line back to Takata. I feel we all have our own direct connection to the divine essence of Reiki, we bring in our individualized presence of this divine light and love and therefore there is little need to focus on how many steps the student is from the master. We are all masters in our own right and I honor that in myself and in others.

My Reiki instruction was brief yet the experience was transformational. After five days in Germany, I returned to American soil, happy to be home and clear as to my next step. I did not feel mass amounts of energy moving in my hands, I really did not feel any sensations when I placed my hands on another but that did not matter. In my heart I knew I was given the gift to teach others and share the process of healing and personal empowerment. I had never taught and knew little of healing, yet it all seemed right. I was stepping into the apparent flow the Universe had set up for me and I felt at peace.

I share my story so others, who feel drawn to Reiki for no apparent reason, follow their guidance. We do not choose Reiki, it chooses us. This gift emerges when we most need it and it materializes to those who are searching. Reiki is a base; it is not the be all and end all. It is a starting point. Not all who learn Reiki will become practitioners or teachers but all who learn will profit. I have seen the change in so many people, there is no doubt in my mind as to the power of Reiki. It led me to open my own healing center called Light Internal, where I provide treatments and teach about Reiki and other forms of personal awakening, to those who seek it. More information about my philosophy and classes can be found at LightInternal.com where you can sign up for my free monthly newsletter.

I suggest you step into this healing modality with an open mind and it will open your heart. Follow the voice in your heart and your advancement will be granted. I cannot tell you where it will take you or how long the journey will be. All I can say is you will be transformed. Once you step into Reiki you will never be the same. If you do not want to change, close this book now and read no further. If you are looking for your truth then proceed.

This book holds the light so you may uncover your path and your power.

I bless you on your journey.

Marnie Vincolisi, Tucson, Arizona *2010*

Chapter 1

The Gift of Reiki

The word *Reiki* is pronounced "ray key." The simplest way to remember the name is to visualize a ray of light flowing into the body and opening the heart with a key, thus Reiki (ray key.) It is an energy which, when activated and summoned, flows from the Universe into the top of the head (crown chakra), enters into the heart (heart chakra) and then flows out through the chakras in the hands. It channels in the essence of all that is and therefore uses the healing energy of pure divine love. Love is nonjudgmental and available to anyone who asks for it and so is Reiki. It is an energetic ray of violet light that unlocks the heart as it enters the crown chakra and flows through the body. This energy flow is not contingent upon any religious beliefs or dogmas; anyone of any consciousness can use it with complete success. Its flowing Japanese translation reflects this.

Reiki is universal life force energy.
Rei means: Universal
                    Transcendent spirit
                    Mysterious power
                    Essence

Ki means: Life force energy, similar to:
                    chi in Chinese spiritual practices
                    light in Christian practice
                    prana in Sanskrit
                    bioplasmic energy in Russian energy healing

~ *Reiki is love, pure and simple* ~

There is a healing power within each of us that can be activated at anytime. It can automatically be used when we are in pain.

Example: When we are hurt, we instinctively place our hands upon the injured area to ease the pain. Our innate sense tells us that there is some kind of energy force in our hands that makes us feel better. This "something" is our own natural healing energy, called *Reiki*.

Through a specific *attunement* process, this universal energy is amplified to an amazing degree. The *attunement* process is what differentiates Reiki from other healing modalities. Other energy techniques teach the student to feel and to use their healing energy. Reiki actually initiates this energy immediately via the *Reiki attunement allowing the student to feel the energy almost instantaneously.*

The *Reiki attunement* is an ancient spiritual process, which increases the natural healing energy held within the body. During the attunement process, the chakras in the head, heart, and hands are opened, allowing the universal life force to course through the body stronger than it has previously. Chakras are

etheric energy centers, which anchor and radiate out from the spine. They filter how information is perceived in the mind and body. More information on chakras will be discussed in the following chapters.

When this ancient procedure is performed, unusual and unexplainable things occur. The experience is unique for each student, but often something miraculous happens. The gift of Reiki quickly raises the energy vibration of the student, elevating them from the spiritual place where they reside into a much higher plane. Whether the student has studied metaphysics or is a complete novice is immaterial; every participant has an enormous energy surge. Initiates often comment that during the attunement process they have an awareness of a presence near them, but it is not the master doing the attunement, for they can hear the master attuning someone in another part of the room. After the attunement colors may appear more vibrant. The initiate may recognize an expanded feeling in their crown chakra, a tingling sensation in their hands, all-over energized vibrations or the experience of a profound love.

Reiki can heal at a very deep level because it addresses issues not only in the physical body but also in the three other bodies found in the etheric field. These are the spiritual, mental and emotional bodies. To heal at the deepest level, one needs to work out issues that reside in all of these bodies. Reiki touches the physical body, thus relieving physical symptoms such as stress and pain, but it reaches out to uncover the mysteries hidden in the other bodies as well. To reveal how the mental and emotional bodies are affected you will find the all inclusive research of Louise Hay in *Heal Your Body*.

There she describes how emotions are reflected in the physical form. She lists numerous physical ailments and conditions and describes the emotional and mental connections to them. Apply her information to your own life experiences and see if this information resonates for you. The information contained in Hay's book is usually right on the money. If it is not precise to the emotions associated with the person, it will at least open the reader to entertain a new perspective on the situation.

The beauty of Reiki is that it always works despite any resistance that might be present. It works even if an individual's belief system does not support it. For Reiki is guided by the higher self of the individual receiving the gift of Reiki and this love will always enter and bless the person.

There is no need to enter a meditative state to give Reiki effectively, though the energy of Reiki does create a very relaxed state in the client as well as the practitioner. The difference between Reiki and other healing practices is with Reiki once a student is attuned to Reiki, their healing ability will never be lost or diminished, even if they do not use it frequently. Once one is opened to the universal flow of Reiki energy, it will always be accessible.

The process of doing Reiki is quite simple: one only needs to ask for the universal energy to enter into their body and it will begin to flow. From there, by visualizing the energy, one can direct Reiki into the body by placing their hands on themselves or another person. The energy is all-knowing and will find the place in the body where it is required; no intuitive direction is necessary. Even without a lot of practice one can apply this energy with great success and the practitioner does not need to believe in the ability of Reiki to have it work.

The following is a true story about a man who was not a religious man. He was not involved in any metaphysical studies and knew nothing about Reiki at the time.

John suffered from arthritis for ten years and was medicated for ongoing back pain. He made a conscious decision to decrease his medication but did not know how he would accomplish this. His intent created an energetic change and he sought Reiki. He traveled from Los Angeles to Denver and received two Reiki treatments. After the treatments, his pain subsided and he returned to Los Angeles.

One week later, John shared that his back pain had returned. He was told that Reiki energy could be sent across the miles without actually applying the hands-on technique. He was reluctant to try this technique, not understanding

how the pain could be alleviated without direct touching, but skeptically agreed to have a distant, hands-off treatment.

Several days later John called, this time asking about the side effects of Reiki. It seems that the day after receiving distant Reiki he felt tenderness in his back, which lasted for four days. He described the feeling as resembling sunburn that was very sensitive to touch. After the fourth day the tender sensation disappeared, along with the recurring back pain.

John was so impressed with his pain relief that he learned Reiki so he could continue with treating himself. Reiki is one of the few healing modalities where self-treatment is easy and effective. John now controls his arthritic inflammation by using this ancient technique. He is able to greatly reduce his pain medication when he uses Reiki. John found that a self Reiki treatment every few days sufficiently reduces his painful arthritis.

Besides self-directed healing, the energy can also be given to another person, an animal, a plant and even inanimate objects such as electronic equipment or traffic. It balances and redirects energy so its use is unlimited.

Even young children have enhanced their inherent healing abilities with a Reiki class and attunement. When children learn Reiki it becomes a way to honor the natural intuitive gifts of these blessed little spirits. It will often help them cope with the sometimes unbalanced world in which they live.

Because Reiki is the energy of love, the process cannot be done incorrectly, nor can it cause harm. There is no wrong way to give Reiki, for it is channeling the universal energy which encompasses the earth and sky. It does not have a religious origin. Therefore, anyone of any belief system may benefit from it.

Reiki is a very simple process. All one needs to do is request the universal energy, place their hands on themselves or on another person and the healing flows. One is not drained of energy because as the practitioner you are not using your energy to do the healing. The healing energy comes from a higher source and flows into and through your body and out your hands. It can be seen as divine assistance coming from the higher self, the spirit of the universe or simply the love which radiates in the earth, because it draws from the oneness which connects us to everyone and every living thing.

A Reiki practitioner allows the healing energy, light, or love, to flow through their hands and into their body or the body of another. In this way we are healing at a core level, because we are healing through love. This love can come from another being, but ultimately when we heal at the deepest level we are healing through self-love. When healing occurs, the patient has opened their heart to permit the medication, medical practice or alternative care to work. When we heal, we are allowing the love of the universe to flow into our bodies, promoting healing us at the core level, which is often held by the emotions.

To help us understand how emotions affect the physical afflictions of the body, Karol Truman, author of *Feelings Buried Alive Never Die*, explains in detail how this all comes together. The book lists our body ailments and the emotions that are often tied to each particular disorder. The underlying cause of an illness can stem from any of the four bodies: physical, mental, emotional or spiritual. If the disorder is allowed to remain there long enough, it will eventually take form as "dis-ease" in the physical body, giving the afflicted person an opportunity to look at the deeper cause. The term "dis-ease" refers to a body being ill-at-ease, rather than diseased. Using this term allows the person to take responsibility for what is occurring in the body. We are not victims of our circumstances—we are the creators of them.

Unfortunately, our society does not teach us how to recognize the messages of dis-ease. We have not been taught to listen to our bodies' rhythms; therefore, we often miss the signals that could potentially alarm us so that adjustments could be made before part of the body's systems shut down. Here lies the importance of a reference book such as Truman's.

Allopathic (conventional) medical treatments only affect the physical body and serve as a Band-Aid to the underlying problem. They do not address the

underlying origin of dis-ease because the treatment does not identify the emotional or mental triggers. In order to truly heal, one must be willing to look within oneself for the map to recovery. Reiki greatly aids this process by creating an awareness of the emotional blocks that caused the distress or dis-ease in the first place.

How does this happen? The effect of Reiki is powerful, yet very subtle. If one does not pay attention, changes can happen and they may go totally unnoticed by the untrained person. Observing the quiet thoughts that surface in one's mind can reveal emotional blocks.

Example: The memory of a distressing childhood incident may resurface. The incident may have been forgotten and is now being recalled because it needs to be addressed in a new light. There is no need to meditate on it for hours. Just evoke the memory from a new adult perspective in a place of forgiveness and compassion, where it can be let go. Reiki softens the heart and helps to open the doorways to new understandings that come from a place of love. Even the worst abuser can be seen in a new light, through the healing love that transpires with Reiki. This hands-on technology opens the heart of the receiver and corresponding chakras where intuition is accessed. Knowledge is gained, compassion for old situations is granted and old energy is given permission to clear and leave.

Very often this compassion is found by forgiving ourselves. Adults who live in pain often blame themselves for their hardships. In most instances, they become harder on themselves than on others. The reason people do not become still and sit with their emotions is that they are afraid of what might be unleashed. There is a compassionate light that leads us to self-discovery. It will never reveal more than can be processed.

~ Life does not give us any more than we can handle ~

There may be challenging times in one's life when painful memories surface. They will not disappear unless they are addressed. The anxiety these thoughts generate can be alleviated with the assistance of the angels and other "light" beings. These transcendent beings live to serve. They wait for your call for help and support. Since Reiki is a healing form of light, it opens the doorway to these great beings and arranges a victorious walk through disturbing past issues.

There is an attunement in Reiki that connects the initiate to a channel of pure divine love. This love can heal distress; astonishingly its energy, once found, will never be lost. Once the pathway is opened it will never close down, though sometimes the student feels the energy is gone because of lack of use. This is never the case. The healing abilities of Reiki never go away.

There is not a need to enter a deep state of meditation to use the healing powers of Reiki, though the dynamics of Reiki will almost create that state all on their own. If one does meditate, they will find that their contemplations will deepen as they will have the ability to enter a quiet state more quickly than before opening to Reiki.

When requested, Reiki will begin its descent from the universe as it enters the head of the practitioner. The energy travels to the heart and then to the hands. When our hands are placed on our own body or that of someone else, the energy starts to flow. First it will move through the practitioner and then into the receiver. The higher selves of all of those involved are directing it. The higher self of the Reiki healer opens the channel for the healing to flow. The higher self of the receiver directs the love to the place of greatest need, which may be physical, mental, emotional or spiritual. The divine intelligence knows what is needed thus relieving the practitioner of the responsibility of its effect.

Reiki energy flows into and through the body of the practitioner and because the practitioner does not use any of their own vital life force in the process, they are not drained of their personal energy. In fact, the practitioner also receives the benefits of Reiki while giving a treatment. Often the practitioner finds they are energized at the end of the process.

The healing of Reiki goes out to all life every time it is used. This becomes an enormous blessing for the planet. Certainly, it is good for us to contribute to the healthy ecology of our environment by recycling paper and plastic, but how about recycling healing energy and sending it out to all life? The greater the number of people who know and use Reiki, the more the consciousness of the planet is raised. This is how healing can be expanded to and through the entire planet with very little effort.

Reiki comes from a universal source of oneness and is extremely powerful. It does not interfere with traditional medical treatments; it actually enhances herbs, medications and medical procedures and restores energy while one is ill or in recovery. Because the practitioner is a channel for the healing energy, it's essential to exercise caution and not allow their personal desires to interfere with the treatment. One cannot wish someone well. The receiver and others who are close may need to experience the process of the illness. The healer should channel the energy and then step aside from any expectations. Accept no credit or blame for the outcome. An outsider may be unaware of the life challenges a client must experience for his or her spiritual growth. Be cognizant that the healing or lack thereof, can be for the client's highest soul purpose.

When you acquire the ability to channel the universal life force in your hands, learn to use it frequently, especially on yourself. Reduce the use of over-the-counter drugs and use Reiki instead. At the sign of a cold, use an alternative natural approach and give yourself a few self-treatments during the days you feel ill-at-ease. If a headache arises, slow down and reach for self-healing before getting the bottle of aspirin. When stressed, emotionally distraught or angry, try Reiki first. When a student takes the role of healer, all eyes will be upon them. One must walk their talk in order for others to truly trust them as a practitioner. In this way you become the example.

Reiki is pure love and as it flows through the body of the giver, it begins to change their life.

Example: There was one Reiki student who found during the first week of learning Reiki his nightly bottle of beer no longer appealing. People who enjoy sugar find sweetness is flowing into their life in other forms and the desire for excess sugar becomes reduced. An individual who allows angry thoughts to control his driving will now become calmer, all after a few Reiki treatments or an attunement.

Why the change? Because when universal love flows into the body the vibration is raised and everything in life becomes altered by this vibrational shift. Friends, employment, the home environment--all may change if they no longer resonate in the new vibratory field of the initiate. These changes may be unnerving at first but soon the student will adjust. The modifications begin to take effect and often, the student surprisingly finds that life is flowing much better than before, almost as if their inner desires are heard and the Universe is responding by eliminating the unnecessary bulk.

There are times when people are in our lives who really don't serve us, yet it is difficult to release them. The student will find these unbalanced acquaintances drop away and new ones who are in tune with their higher frequency step in. The job that pays the bills but does not feed the spirit will almost magically disappear and a new job will appear to replace it. This is what happened when I began to receive the message to close my toy business and find a new vocation. These changes are a result of the new energetic frequency of the physical, mental, and emotional bodies.

Reiki can be used anytime or anywhere for:
- Pain relief
- Stress relief
- Quick energy
- Protection of your personal space in airplanes, auto, at work, etc.

Reiki:

- Flows through and opens the chakras
- Flows through energy blocks, breaks them up and helps dissolve them
- Brings up emotional issues so they can be understood and released, which allows for emotional and spiritual growth
- Raises the body's vibratory rate

Benefits of Reiki

1. Self-treatment. Reiki is one of the few healing modalities which facilitates self-healing.
2. Total relaxation.
3. New perspectives.
4. Release of buried emotions and energy blocks.
5. Physical healing.
6. Balancing and emanating love into the body.

Once one commits to learning Reiki, personal growth rapidly increases. From this moment, one is empowered to take charge. Even before the first attunement, there are Reiki guides who provide assistance. They start by rearranging things in your life, moving out the old, which no longer serves, and bringing in the new. Observe this for yourself: once on the path of Reiki, take a moment to look back and see how things have changed since the decision was made to learn Reiki. Sometimes the change is immediate, within days and weeks, but it continues to expand as it reaches all facets of life. To get a better perspective on how you are advancing look back several months ago and to the past year and contemplate the inevitable changes. You may be surprised at what you find. For most, the change is obvious; for others it is more subtle. Reiki opens one to be more aware. It enters subtly, but with discernment the changes begin to become apparent.

You have been chosen to receive the gift of Reiki. You may think that you made the decision to learn and practice Reiki. However, know that you did not choose Reiki, Reiki chose you. Yes, you must want to accept the gift but know you were chosen by a higher source to receive this blessing. Step back and honor who you are and accept the radiance bestowed upon you.

Students who learn and practice Reiki find their self confidence increases. They find their inner power and have the new ability to maintain deep sense of peace. It is easier to be emotionally balanced when dealing with difficult situations. New perspectives are seen as old triggers are eased and control of their live beings to come into play. There is a sense of being unaffected by the negativity of others. Reiki really does change your life.

The Principles of Reiki

Just for today
do not worry

Just for today
do not anger

Honor your parents
teachers and elders

Earn your living
honestly

Show gratitude to
every living thing

The energy reflected in Reiki is not new to the planet, it has been with us since the beginning of time. It has been known by many different names, such as *hands-on healing* or the *laying on of hands,* as it is spoken of in the Bible. Reiki is similar to the healing work of Jesus and Buddha, in that it comes from a higher source, not necessarily the giver. Jesus healed by seeing people in the divine perfection which they possessed. Is that not the purest form of love? Buddha instilled the oneness of life and how we are all connected. This connection is what gives us the ability to transfer the healing love found in Reiki to another. It is an ancient technology for fine-tuning the physical and etheric bodies to a higher vibratory frequency so that we can get in touch with our inner essence.

Mikao Usui (1865-1926) rediscovered this natural healing technique in the late 1800s. His story had been handed down by word of mouth so there are a few different versions of this story. The following is the Christian version.

While Dean at Doshisha University, a small Christian university in Kyoto, Japan, Dr. Usui's students asked him how Jesus healed. The students wanted to know why, with all the knowledge they received, they could not heal as Jesus did. Dr. Usui could not answer this question and it compelled him to search for the answer. His quest would last more than 20 years.

Unable to find an answer in Japan, Dr. Usui traveled to the United States, where he studied at a theological seminary at the University of Chicago. He did not find any teachings on the healing techniques used by Jesus and he found this was not to be an easy quest. Still determined to find the answer, he traveled back to his homeland of Japan, this time to a Buddhist monastery.

Dr. Usui knew that Buddha had had the ability to heal, so he thought that surely the Buddhist monks would also have this gift. The monks responded that in the past they had indeed had the ability to heal, but that this gift had been lost

due to lack of use. Their focus had been primarily on healing of the spirit and so the ability to heal the body had become lost.

Finally, at a Zen monastery, Dr. Usui began to search through the Sanskrit Sutras of Tibet. Within these Sutras he found the information he desired. He discovered healing techniques and methods for applying them. However, much to his surprise, he still did not have the ability to heal. Unable to figure out why, Dr. Usui confided in his friend, the Abbot of the monastery. Together they came to the conclusion that Dr. Usui should meditate on Mount Kuri Yama, the holy mountain of Kyoto and ask for the ability to heal.

His experience followed an age-old tradition similar to the experience in a Native American practice called "vision questing." When young native boys reach the age of puberty, they venture away from the tribe to find their true purpose in life. Once their direction is revealed, they continue throughout their life to go into the silence of vision questing to acquire added knowledge and support for their soul purpose. This quest follows the pattern of four days, ten days, twenty one days and forty days.

Spiritual seekers have practiced this technique for eons. Even Jesus did his own form of questing. When he went into the thicket to pray he stayed there for forty days. He was searching for knowledge and knew that in order to find the information, he must be in solitude. Usui followed the path of some of the Buddhist monks he had met and left his home to pray upon the mountain for 21 days.

Near the end of his quest, unfortunately Usui was still no closer to having the ability to heal, for no information had been presented to him in thought or dreams. On the last day, early in the moonless morning, the sky was quite dark, but the answer was soon to be presented. Stones were kept in the questing circle to keep track of the days that passed. As Dr. Usui threw the last of the 21 stones out of his circle, he sent out a prayer to God that he be granted the gift to heal.

As he looked up into the dark sky, Usui saw a star which was particularly bright. His intuition told him this star had consciousness. The transmission began as Usui listened to the star: it told him he could receive the ability to heal, but the energy transfer was so strong that it could kill him upon contact. His first inclination was to run for his life. His second thought was to stay still and receive whatever was going to happen. After all, he had been searching for an answer for so long, surely he could not turn away now, even if it were to mean death. With that thought, a ball of bright light came streaming toward him and as the light hit him in the third eye, it knocked him to the ground. In his altered state he began to see beautiful bubbles of light raining over him. Within the bubbles of light were three-dimensional symbols in glittering gold.

When Usui awoke, he found that he was not dead only unconscious for quite some time, as the sun was now high in the sky. Excitement filled his whole being as he ran down the mountain, eager to speak to his friend in the monastery. Little did he know that soon three miracles would occur. He was amazed at how much energy he had, even though he had not eaten for three weeks.

In his haste, his footing was not steady; he tripped and painfully injured his toe against a large rock. He looked down to find that his toenail was torn back and his toe was bleeding profusely. His natural instincts were to reach down and hold the toe. Much to his amazement, when he removed his hand both bleeding and pain had ceased. This was the first miracle of the morning.

Usui continued his descent down the mountain and passed through a small town. The villagers were accustomed to observing the monks who regularly meditated on Mount Kuri Yama. They could tell by Usui's gruff appearance that he had been on the mountain for quite some time. One family invited him into their home to partake of some broth. Usui saw a full meal on their table and asked to have this food as well. The family was reluctant, as Usui had not eaten for three weeks and his digestion would surely rebel. All were gladly surprised to see Usui could eat and enjoy a huge meal while not suffering any indigestion after his long fast. This was the second miracle.

Dr. Usui heard someone crying in a back room, where he found a young girl who was very uncomfortable from a toothache. She had no relief because the family was poor and could not afford medical care. Usui decided to try his newfound skill to see if he could ease her pain, as he had done on his own torn toenail. The third miracle was performed as the pain subsided and the swelling in her jaw was reduced.

Usui returned to the monastery only to find his old friend, the monk, lying in bed, unable to walk from arthritis. When Usui placed his hands upon the arthritic areas, both friends felt the energy charging through. The monk's pain disappeared and he was able to walk again. Now Usui was puzzled. What should he do with his newfound skill? Where is the greatest need?

The monk's advice to Usui was that he should go to the Beggar's Quarter of Kyoto to help heal the poor. He immediately left to serve in this manner and practiced there for seven years, until one day he noticed a beggar who looked familiar. He inquired as to how he might have known this man and the beggar replied that he had been healed by Usui years before. The custom of the monks was to bring beggars who had been healed to the temple, give them a name and show them ways to work for wages. The man had been working and raising a family, but he had found working too hard. He thought begging was much easier, so he had returned to the streets.

This event greatly disturbed Usui, so to find solace he entered into deep meditation, asking what had gone wrong. He discovered that by giving away his healing ability, he had been encouraging the beggars to continue their pattern of receiving without being responsible for giving in return. Usui was on a one-way street. He gave as others received. The circle was never complete. The law of the universe has ebb and flow--what goes out comes back. This circle had been broken. Usui had not honored the idea that even a beggar possesses something of value, which could have been given in return. He also saw that what the monks said was true: it is not enough to heal just the body. One must also attend to the spirit. While in deep contemplation, Usui was gifted with what we now call the two precepts of Reiki.

In order for the highest good to come of Reiki, Mikao Usui determined that:

1. The individual should ask for healing.
2. There should be an exchange of energy for the healer's time.
   - Therefore, do not give Reiki away. Honor that the receiver has something of value to give back to you.
   - If they are unable to reciprocate, know the Universe will create the balance in ways you would not expect.
   - Be open to receiving your gift in return.
   - By giving Reiki away, one sets up an imbalance where the receiver feels indebted for services rendered.
   - Accepting a gift (in any form) frees the giver of further obligation.
   - Exchange does not always need to be monetary.

The beginning student can lose clarity on these two precepts. First, let the person in need know about the healing gift which has been bestowed upon you. Until you inform them, they will not know that you hold this special ability and will not ask for it. Therefore, let others know that you possess a skill that eases pain on the physical and emotional levels. Intuition will tell you how to approach the subject with each individual. Some will be comfortable knowing it is God's healing hands working through you; others will accept it to be an all-knowing Universal light. The simplest way to explain this phenomenon is to call it love. When others are in pain, usually they do not care what is making them feel better as long it does. So don't hold back; the worst that can happen is that they will refuse the help. There will always be another time and opportunity to suggest the gift of Reiki again.

~ When one comes from their heart
all things are possible ~

Dr. Usui decided to spread the word of Reiki only to those who would ask for healing. He did this by carrying a torch through the streets of Kyoto. The villagers were curious as to why he was carrying a torch in daylight. He told them the torch was a symbol of the light of the spirit and if they wanted to know more they should come to a talk that he was giving that night. The people would come and he would teach Reiki to them upon their request. This is the traditional version of how Reiki came to be spread among the people.

It has been over 100 years since Usui has channeled Reiki and perhaps the story has been embellished over the years. The second version of the story of Dr. Usui is quite interesting. Apparently there is no record of Dr. Usui having been a student at the University of Chicago or receiving his degree in theology. Nor is there any record of his having been the dean of Doshisha University, the Christian school in Kyoto, Japan, thus dispelling the Christian influence on Reiki. These controversies only support the idea that one needs to find their personal truth and not be led and governed by others. Though healing abilities can be taught and transferred, true accolades must be found within one's own being and claimed. Reiki holds a key but it is you who needs to find the door which aligns with your path. Reiki opens the awareness to perceive your gifts and sustains you as a leader, not a follower.

Reiki was introduced to the United States in the 1950s when relations were not at their best between the U.S. and Japan. Mrs. Takata, the Master who brought Reiki to the United States, presented Dr. Usui's background in a Christian light. Mrs. Takata did so in order to make Reiki more palatable to Americans during a time when relations with Japan were shaky. The truth may reveal that Dr. Usui may have been a Buddhist monk and Reiki may have some Tibetan origin. In this way, many cultures are honored, for if Reiki is indeed channeling universal light, then it would need to encompass all people. More of the mysterious background of Usui may be explored in Frank Arjava Petter's book *Reiki Fire*.

William Lee Rand is a Reiki Master who studied in Hawaii under masters who were trained by Takata. He claims that, when Dr. Usui studied the Sanskrit

Sutras, he did not find specific information about Reiki or Reiki symbols. According to Rand, Dr. Usui merely found a formula for contacting the higher power that would bring on healing abilities. The symbols and information on how to use them were given to him during his spiritual experience on Mount Kuri Yama. It is also understood that Usui did have a spiritual experience upon the mountain and was gifted with healing abilities from a star.

It is believed Dr. Usui did Reiki purely by intuition and did not follow any specific form. He attuned his masters all at once, with no levels of certification or breaks in the process. During Dr. Usui's life he attuned sixteen masters, one of whom was Dr. Chujiro Hayashi, a retired naval officer who was attuned as a master in 1925. Dr. Hayashi founded the Reiki clinic in Tokyo. Dr. Hayashi was proficient in martial arts and appreciated the order of levels as they were taught. He developed the three levels of Reiki and the hand positions. He felt that the levels in Reiki would also be a good idea. So, Hayashi was the one who created the structure of Reiki education as we know it today.

In 1935, Hawayo Takata, a Japanese woman from Hawaii, came to Dr. Hayashi's Reiki Clinic in Japan for help with her many medical disorders. Through treatments and healing, she developed a strong interest in Reiki. She spent a long time persuading Dr. Hayashi to teach her the healing art of Reiki. He was very resistant, as Mrs. Takata would be returning to practice Reiki in Hawaii.

Hayashi had seen a decline in the quality of practice and discipline of various martial arts when they were allowed to leave Japan. He did not want the same thing to happen to Reiki. He finally recognized that Takata would not go away so he finally consented and taught her Reiki. She was attuned as a master teacher in 1938. Revealing his wisdom was timely, as the war killed every Reiki master in Japan, and Dr. Hayashi passed on as well but not because of the war. Mrs. Takata, safe in Hawaii, was the only Reiki master left. More information on this fascinating woman can be found on the web or in *Reiki: A Torch in Daylight* by Karyn Mitchell or in *Reiki: The Healing Touch* by William Lee Rand.

Master Takata placed a $10,000 price tag on the Reiki master training. She wanted to be sure Americans would respect and honor the discipline of Reiki. She knew that, in America, money was greatly valued, so she surmised that charging a high fee for Reiki training would surely give it the honor and respect it deserved. She set the fee for Reiki I at $250.00 and for Reiki II at $500. Mrs. Takata's fee structure continues to be used by many traditional Reiki Masters today.

Traditional and Non-Traditional Reiki

Those who continue in the direct lineage of Master Takata teach traditional Reiki. Those who have been given the gift of Reiki through masters who are not from the Usui lineage teach non-traditional Reiki. Both share the same concepts, teach the same symbols and have the same high vibrational frequency. Having experienced both traditional and non-traditional methods, I can attest that they indeed have equal power.

I embrace the non-traditional approach to Reiki because I feel we all have our personal connection to the divine light and love of Reiki. We have walked this land and traversed the cosmos in dreams, meditation and spiritual practices. From our experiences we are the divine beings we created and this presence must be honored. As a master teacher I empower the student to see and reconnect to their personal gift of Reiki; no two initiates are the same. To feel a healing modality or master is more powerful than you is to give your power away. Reiki is a practice which daily allows you to reaffirm your celestial power and love, while knowing you have the ability to share it with yourself and others.

In the last few years Reiki has expanded at a phenomenal rate. Mikao Usui, Chujiro Hayashi and Hawayo Takata each trained between 13 and 20 master teachers. Now there are thousands of master teachers trained traditionally and non-traditionally. William Lee Rand, master teacher in Michigan, claimed back in 1990 that there were as many as 20,000 masters and 1,000,000 Reiki practitioners throughout the world. One can only presume that the number has greatly increased in the past years. As the vibration of the planet is raised, her inhabitants increase their frequencies also. Learning Reiki is a simple, effective tool to assist one in keeping up with the ever-changing energy of Mother Earth.

In the 1980s a change in planetary consciousness allowed the gift of Reiki to come through without being passed down from one traditional master to another. One touching story about a Reiki practitioner named Brian Sutterfield reflects how Reiki began to be transferred without an attunement from a traditional master.

Brian was a nurse who was not able to afford the cost of $10,000 to become a Reiki master. He had received his first two Reiki degrees and was using this gift while working at a nursing home. He became close to an elderly woman whom he had taken care of for three years. Brian was present with this woman when she passed from her body in the transition called death. At the time of her passing, an angel appeared to him and attuned him to his Reiki master energy. The angel said her name was Liberty and he should go out and teach Reiki to those who are ready, at a reasonable cost. He lovingly began to call his lineage Liberty Reiki.

Another second-degree Reiki practitioner from Texas received a master attunement during her meditation. The master symbol appeared to her; upon sharing these symbols with other Reiki masters, she realized that she had been given the master symbols through her higher self. These experiences were just a few ways non-traditional Reiki began and spread.

Reiki is coming to us through many beautiful forms so that we can render the service needed to raise the planetary vibration at this time and assist mankind. The ones who receive attunements to Reiki are chosen and blessed. As Reiki is shared with others, its value is often perceived as a hidden gift that, now revealed, is a true blessing to all. It brings awareness far greater than one could have imagined. This enlightenment extends into all facets of our lives; it is not only used for healing.

Always remember that even though you may not practice traditional Reiki, you have real healing power, even though you do not have a formal lineage back to Takata. The power of your gift can easily be proven by its use. By your own application, you will prove to yourself the intensity of the gift you possess. There can be no doubt.

Honor It ~ Love It ~ Bless It

Traditional Reiki Masters

Birth	Master Attuned	Passing
Dr. Mikao Usui August 15, 1865	Unknown	March 9, 1926
Dr. Chujiro Hayashi September 15, 1880	1925	May 10, 1940
Mrs. Hawayo Takata December 24, 1900	1935	December 19, 1980

Dr. Mikao Usui   Dr. Chujiro Hayashi   Mrs. Hawayo Takata

There are four levels to a Reiki practice. Some lineages teach only three. The third level traditionally includes both the master symbol activation and the teaching component. Many non-traditional classes split the third level into two parts, allowing the opportunity to become a master without taking the time and expense of becoming a teacher.

Degrees of Reiki

The following is an outline of the classes taught in the Light Internal System of hands-on healing.

First Degree Reiki Outline

- Healing treatment for yourself and others.
- Hand positions.
- Chakra balancing.
- The Reiki Power symbol.
- Guidance and opening of your inner power.
- Opening of the chakras in the head, heart and partially in the hands.
- Attunement to the first level of Reiki.
- Preparation to be a certified Reiki practitioner.
- Activation of the 21-day chakra cleanse which:

- o raises the vibratory rate of your body
- o enhances your personal growth.

Second Degree Reiki Outline
- Attunement which completely opens the chakras in the palms.
- Ability to connect with the chakra system of the recipient.
- Attunement to new symbols to access hidden mental and emotional issues.
- Learn to heal at a distance or into the past or future.
- Square the energy of First Degree Reiki and create a quantum leap in intuitive awareness.
- Receive a pendulum and instructions for its myriad uses.
- Lovingly release unhealthy connections to others via "cords."
- Learn to clear addictions, release spirit attachments and enhance relationships.
- Practice the "Five Tibetan Rites" to keep chakras spinning while you stay and feel younger longer.
- Increased integration of "Higher Self" Consciousness.
- Activation of another 21-day chakra cleansing cycle.

Master Degree
- A review of the symbols and the introduction of new, non-traditional symbols.
- Nine Master Symbols from various lineages.
- Numerous ways to apply the master symbol.
- Process to assist beings who have passed to the next dimension.
- A deeper understanding of how healing light works on a myriad of levels.
- Crystal Energy Transfer Grid: A focus for your guides to increase your personal master energy on a continual basis. Also may be used to give healing to another, 24 hours a day.
- Energetic Release, a process which gives an issue form and then clears it.
  - o Brings the recipient under the umbrella of your Reiki master energy.
  - o Clearly allows the recipient to visualize and process the current disturbance.

- Meditation practices and techniques using Reiki symbols.
- Animal communication.
- Advanced understanding of chakras.
- Sensing and seeing auras.
- Understanding the connection of Reiki to Buddhism.

Master Teacher Degree (CRMT, Certified Reiki Master Teacher)
- Learn to pass the attunements for all degrees of Reiki.
- Attunement to Master Teacher level.
- Outline of all Light Internal system books.
- Clearly defined teaching techniques.
- Correspondence letters, calendars, newsletters and e-zines for marketing.
- How to run a successful business.
- Marketing strategies.
- Online classes, contacts and students.
- Graphic computer slide show presentation for all levels, available.
- Activation of the last 21-day chakra cleaning cycle.

Chapter 2

How Reiki Works

Once one is attuned to the flow of the universal light, channeling the energy is easy. All it takes is the request. The universe will not deny a call for help. Reiki is love, pure and simple. Open your heart and let it flow. Because the practitioner is a channel for the healing energy to flow through, they are rewarded for their service by receiving healing during the process. There is an automatic protection which does not allow negativity to be transferred from the giver to the receiver, or vice versa.

Guidance is clearly directed from the higher self of the receiver to the practitioner. It may come in an audible voice, intuitive images or an inner knowing. Often the practitioner places their hands in a location, not knowing why and the receiver responds positively to the touch. Hands-on healing is a practice that instructs the participants to honor and be in the flow. Don't ask why, just do as guided. There are hand positions to follow, which assure that the client will feel that every part of the body has been addressed, but the truth of the matter is this: it does not matter where your hands are placed; the healing will go exactly where it is needed. The positions are guidelines, but they do not need to be followed precisely.

Because love has no limits, when the healing energy begins to flow from the higher self into the head, heart and hands of the practitioner, it continues to send love out to all life. If you are at work, everyone in the building is receiving some of the energy. At home pets will be found entering a room where energy is being channeled, for they are following their instincts and they know they are being aided by this frequency. In relationship your partner will receive Reiki light just by being in your presence, they are then blessed on all levels as well.

Reiki works at the deepest level, because it travels to the core issues stemming from the etheric as well as the physical bodies. The etheric bodies are as far as 18 inches out from the physical body and encompass three bodies: the mental body, the emotional body and the spiritual body. We are more than a physical being and are aware when one of these unseen bodies are compromised. We become uncomfortable when someone steps into these invisible bodies uninvited.

Example: Remember a time when someone came over and talked to you and stood too close. Part of the reason you felt uneasy was that they had entered your personal space, which harbors your emotions, mental knowledge and spiritual presence. If deep healing is going to occur, these bodies cannot be ignored.

This may seem questionable, but Reiki always works 100% of the time, even if no adjustments are apparent. Each body—physical, mental, emotional and spiritual—becomes aware of the healing differently. The results may not always be sensed in the physical body.

The mental, emotional, and spiritual bodies are more personal in their content and the client may not share or even understand their observations. It is important to let go of how the healing *should* occur. Too often one judges the

results of their efforts by the effects portrayed. The human form is a complex organism; therefore, not all of the responses will be seen and understood immediately. Patience, trust and the ability to let go and move into the flow are paramount. An energy practitioner is not responsible for how the client receives and uses the energy channeled; we are free-will beings and that freedom must be given to all. The changes may be sensed in the other bodies where the results are not visible to the physical eye. Be assured, there are still changes happening.

As a practitioner when giving Reiki, you are never drained of your own energy.

- You are a channel for the energy (light.)
- The practitioner does not take on any of the client's problems or issues. The client does not take on any of the practitioner's misgivings.
- The Reiki comes from the all-knowing client's higher self and the client's body will draw the amount of energy required to the part of his or her body where it is most needed.
- The practitioner becomes energized through the process and also receives healing during the treatment.

When Reiki energy flows through the body it flows out to all life.

- It raises the energy of the planet and her inhabitants whether human, animal, mineral or vegetation.
- Become aware of the magnitude of Reiki and extend it with intent to bless and flow out to all life.

Reiki can be used on:

- 🌀 People.
- 🌀 Plants (e.g. to remove insects in the garden rather than using pesticides.)
- 🌀 Animals (e.g. placing hands on a dog's hip so he may walk without pain.)
- 🌀 Objects (e.g. Reiki your books and gifts before you give them to others thus filling them with love.)

Etheric Body

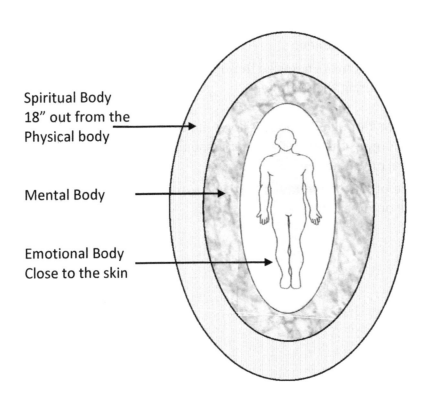

Spiritual Body
18" out from the
Physical body

Mental Body

Emotional Body
Close to the skin

Reiki works on all four bodies:
1. Physical body.
2. Emotional body, located a few inches off the skin.
3. Mental body, between the emotional and spiritual bodies.
4. Spiritual body, as far out as the finger tips when the arms are extended.

Thus, healing is complete because it will be achieved at the deepest level by addressing distress in all of the above bodies.

~ *Reiki cannot be performed incorrectly* ~

1. It cannot be used to harm anyone.
2. It is loving energy directed by the higher self.
3. Once you are attuned to the energy, it will never diminish. Your connection to Reiki will never cease.
4. Reiki flows even when you are not aware of it.
   a. The energy flows whenever you touch yourself or another.
   b. The energy can flow through your eyes as you look out at life.

Reiki works on the cause of disease when you are willing to:
1. Look at the underlying cause.
2. Make the proper changes so healing can occur.

Guidance:
1. You may ask for direction from your guides or higher self.
2. Scripts in this book are only suggestions.
3. Always follow your own inner voice. This is the voice of your divine self directing you.

Results:

- Reiki works 100 % of the time.
- We do not determine what will be the most positive outcome of our work.
- Sometimes lessons need to be learned through illness.
- Practice non-attachment to the results of the healing.

~ Honor yourself and the gift you have been given ~

Attunements

The attunement is an energy transfer channeled from the Reiki master teacher to the initiate. It opens the crown chakra at the top of the head so that the love of the Universe will flow freely into the practitioner. It also opens the heart chakra, reacquainting the participant to the connection they have always had to the love that is ever flowing, in the earth and in their body. In this first level of Reiki, the chakras in the initiates' hands are partially opened to the healing love, which may be given to themselves and others. The second level of Reiki fully opens the chakras in the hands which tremendously increases the energy flow.

Once the opening of the crown chakra occurs in the attunement, the initiates may feel tingling in their head, buzzing in their hands or warmth all over. The master teacher will direct symbols into the head, heart and hands of the initiate to start this process. Some feel the presence of a being over them, even after the master teacher has moved on. Colors can become very vivid during and after the attunement procedure. Each individual experiences the energy transfer in a different way. The preceding are only a few examples of what has been noticed in the past; the variations of experiences are endless. Enter into the ceremony of

the attunement without expectations and be open to how the Universe will gift you. Let it be a surprise.

The attunement can also be given remotely, without the physical presence of the master teacher. It is my observation that an attunement at a distance can have the same intensity as when performed in person. Reiki is energy, it travels through the air unseen, like electricity, and its transforming power is observed and felt as it opens and illumines the initiate. A Reiki treatment can also be given remotely by a practitioner and this process will be covered in the second degree Reiki manual.

A remote attunement can be performed via the phone or with an online computer service which allows the student and teacher to see each other with a web cam while speaking to each other over the internet. I have found the student can have the similar experiences as the student does who is sitting before me.

Example: Pam, a new student who was receiving a remote attunement was skeptical at first for she was uninformed about the process of Reiki and could not understand how the energy of Reiki could be transferred without the physical presence of a master teacher. As the attunement began she was surprised how calm her body became within just a few minutes and she began to observe beautiful colors with her inner sight. Her crown began to buzz and her hands became very warm. All of this was expected but delightedly received.

Reiki transcends space and time, it is pure energy, pure love. With a clear intent of the student and master, the attunement has all the divine qualities of the attunement given in the presence of the master teacher and is everlasting. It can be beneficial to give an attunement to an animal or a small child.

Example: There was once a cat that lived on a 25 acre ranch; this land was carrying some of the negative energy from the Indians who once lived there. This sweet animal was empathic to mother earth and the ancestors who had lived there long ago. I spoke to this pet and told him it was not necessary for him to clear the land through his body. I attuned him so he would be aware of how to channel energy. He lay still during the attunement and when it was complete he seemed to know. He jumped off the couch and ran around the room obviously feeling something. He responded in a similar way when I would give him a full hour Reiki treatment. Intuitively he would know when the treatment was complete.

I will attune newborns and children if there is someone in the family who will support and guide the child in their inherit skill of healing. Children are naturally intuitive but often lose this skill because they are told when they sense the unseen that this sensation is only their imagination. This invalidation can diminish their inner vision over a period of time. The Reiki attunement along with a loving family member will support and increase their natural abilities. I have taught Reiki to children in a class setting as young as six years old but I find eight years old and above is preferable as they have a longer attention span.

Once the attunement process is complete, the difference is often felt immediately in the hands of the initiate. Sometimes, however, the initiate will not feel anything and will question the effect of the attunement. Rest assured, I have yet to see the attunement not work. Even when the student senses nothing in their hands when channeling Reiki, the person receiving the energy always feels something transpiring from the giver. In our society we have been taught to ignore intuitive feelings so many times it may take longer to reverse these teachings. In time, all students will feel the power coming out of their hands and heart.

The Attunement Process

1. Opens the chakras in the crown, in the heart and partially in the hands.

2. Once you are attuned, the healing energy will always be available for sharing.
3. The Reiki attunement is a sacred spiritual initiation which:
   a. connects the initiate with higher levels of consciousness;
   b. opens the initiate to an unlimited source of healing energy.
4. No spiritual or physical purification is required in order for the Reiki attunement to be effective.

The main differences between Reiki and other healing modalities:
1. Reiki opens the crown chakra and connects the practitioner to the Universal energy or higher self at the onset of the attunement.
2. An initiation is rarely given with other practices. The Reiki initiation through the attunement allows the receiver to clear and heal on a personal level.
3. Reiki starts the healing energy flowing immediately.
4. Other modalities may only teach how to get in touch with and feel the energy; Reiki creates a clear connection to the transmitted high vibrations.
5. Through the attunement process, Reiki actually turns on the flow of healing energy and it can be felt immediately.

The 21-Day Cleanse Process

The vibration of the body increases after a student has been attuned to their Reiki energy. This new frequency manifests changes in all aspects of life: personal, family, work and home. Initiates find they are not the same people they were before and everything begins to change. What resonated and felt right before may not seem necessary now. The initiate will find that friends who are not in alignment with the highest good of their spirit may leave; a job they have may dissolve if it no longer serves them; but always new opportunities will arise. Watch with a careful eye; do not let the changes ruffle your feathers. Trust that you are on a path of new discovery and then it becomes fun and exciting.

In order to have clearer intuition, you need to listen to the messages from your higher self. To do this, you need to increase your vibration to achieve the same frequency, so to speak, as this divine intelligence; then their guidance will be sensed. This is accomplished by raising the vibratory level of the body through the attunement and continued self treatments. It is as if the crown chakra becomes a radio station and the initiate is the receiver, able to tune into messages from the Universe. At times the message is loud and clear and at other times a bit fuzzy. By daily administering self Reiki the initiate will continue to bring in an audible channel.

Now that you are attuned to Reiki energy, you have a clear channel to your divine self. By doing Reiki on yourself often, an average of five to seven times a week, you will be keeping this line clear and open. The trick is to listen to your inner guidance, which is that little voice inside your head. Do not dismiss this communication as "just your imagination." It is real and holds valuable information.

During the attunement, the vibratory rate of the physical and etheric bodies are raised very quickly. Old, dense, negative emotions and thoughts are forced to the surface and released. Initiates are now in a new, brighter energetic body. Unbalanced patterns of the past no longer resonate within the new vibratory field, so they begin to release. This "letting go" is accomplished through a physical and energetic cleanse which opens new perceptions to these old issues. The "cleanse" may manifest in different forms for different people. Know these manifestations are not permanent and will pass. Not everyone experiences discomfort during the raising of the vibration of the physical, mental, emotional and spiritual bodies, just be aware that changes may be felt in the following ways.

Physically, you may experience:

- Headaches.
- Tiredness (needing a nap every day.)
- Extra energy (not requiring much sleep.)
- Cold symptoms.
- Flu-like symptoms.
- Stomach upsets.

Mentally you could sense:

- An inability to concentrate.
- Difficulty focusing and staying on task.
- Foggy thinking.

Emotionally there could be:

- Sadness, weeping.
- Joy, love and appreciation for all life.
- Old issues brought to the surface and newly understood.
- Opening up old wounds, triggered by reconnection with old friends or relatives.
- Awareness that things are different.
- Reconnection with old friends.

Spiritually, you may encounter:

- Colors seem brighter and the world appears clearer.
- There is an appreciation of the beauty of nature and a deeper connection to it.
- Renewed awareness of the love which is in every living thing.

Remember, anything disturbing which comes up during the cleanse can be eased by doing Reiki on yourself. Also, the cleanse, like a good massage, may bring toxins up to the surface to be cleared away, so drink plenty of water to lighten any discomfort from the release of these impurities.

Reiki flows through the seven major chakras, so they need to be fully open and functioning for the best action to be received. The 21-day clearing process focuses on these light centers, opening them and allowing Reiki to channel through. In *Anatomy of the Spirit: the Seven Stages of Power and Healing*, Caroline Myss explains the functioning of the chakras in great depth. She describes how these energy centers have been affected since birth and how they connect us to our basic tribal issues and our response to other people. There is a myriad of information that can be found in these etheric energy centers. During meditation, while in the stillness of the mind, information can be accessed. The "Life Tools" found in the following chapters will show how to locate knowledge in these centers and apply it in everyday life.

During the 21-day cleanse, one chakra may be cleansed each day throughout the first week (i.e., seven chakras, seven days.) During the second week, the first chakra is once again cleansed on the eighth day and so on, through all the seven chakras. This continues for three weeks, sweeping each chakra and allowing each one to open and cleanse a total of three times, hence the 21 days. The clearing may start at the base chakra or the crown and can even skip around; there is no absolute pattern.

Another way for the clearing to take place is that one chakra is cleansed for three days before moving to the next. Some have experienced a quick cleanse of twenty minutes at each chakra from head to toe and then the physical sensations ceased. The different ways we process cleansing exist because they reflect the unique individuals we are. By keeping track of which emotions are coming up in a journal, one can see how each clearing is manifesting at a physical, mental, emotional or spiritual level. There is a "cleansing journal" at the end of this book specific for this purpose. Then one can get an idea of what patterns are being diminished though the cleanse.

Nothing needs to be done to activate this cleanse. It occurs naturally as the attunement process increases the vibratory level of the initiate's body. One may think nothing is happening during the 21-day cleanse. However, if the initiate looks back at what was written in their journal, they often discover a pattern emerging. These clues show how they were being changed and fine tuned during this adjustment period.

Reiki clients also go through a mini-cleanse after their treatments. Their process will last about three days and will be less intense than the student's 21 days, but can have similar effects. Reiki treatments continue to work for three days on the more subtle levels. It is wise to explain this clearing process so that the client can receive all the benefits of their session and to be open to new perceptions in the following days.

In *Reiki: a Torch in Daylight*, Karyn Mitchell describes this cleansing process as a detoxifying of your life: a "shaman's death," which allows the student to go far beyond the self. Life does not give us more than we can handle. Though it may not seem so at the time, this opening is a wonderful healing process that elevates the student to heights not yet experienced. Embrace this time, bless it and know this clearing is making way for a more transcendent you. Some students fly through this period with little physical or emotional disturbance; others are more affected. The new vibrations are established in the body, no matter what the experience. The Reiki attunement, like Reiki, is guided by the higher self and is always in divine order.

Example: Cathy, a Reiki student and gifted psychic, had an experience which gives one explanation of how our chakras open and clear during the initial activation of Reiki. While sitting quietly in meditation, she heard a physical popping and then felt energy begin to flow from her base chakra up to her crown. She also heard a vacuum noise, as though she were listening to the sound inside a seashell. Cathy interpreted the popping to be the opening of the chakras and the vacuum to be the cleansing of each chakra.

Opening and cleansing can be experienced in many different ways. Stay aware and try not to discount what is felt no matter how diminished or intense. This will keep intuition open and make the process fun and exciting.

The Process of Using Reiki

The following are only guidelines for using Reiki. Ultimately the practitioner will access their personal healing essence and develop their own style. These suggestions are to get one started. Once the student is familiar and comfortable with the process, individual techniques will arise. Bringing in the healing energy with ease and flowing with joy opens the heart for the practitioner as well as the client. Trusting inner guidance will accelerate the process of discovering the divine gifts held within.

Healing energy is similar to prayer, as the response is instantaneous. The age old phrase, "the call compels the answer," reflects how the transition is complete as soon as the request is sent. So follows the order of Reiki or other healing practices. Healing is the love held in the earth and sky, manifesting through the energetic form of Reiki. The intent to help yourself or another is all that is needed to create the download.

When first beginning to learn how to transfer energy, it is a good idea to get in touch with the *feeling* of the energy. When intent for healing is requested and attention is placed at the crown or heart chakra the light will begin to flow out the palms of the hands. There could be a sensation of heat, coolness, tingling or heaviness. Once the flow of energy is felt, the treatment can begin. The hands are then placed on the body; fingers kept together almost cupping the energy so that it will concentrate itself in one place.

Keep fingers together when transferring energy

Reiki I Guidelines

1. Turn off the phone so your attention will not be redirected.
2. Ask for the Reiki to enter your crown, heart and hand chakras.
3. You have freedom to decide how and where to apply and use healing energy.
4. Be still and listen if there is an inner voice. Follow it, or just proceed and trust the process will work for the highest good of all concerned.

5. Place your hands on the body, fingers touching, slightly curved, and cupping the light. Connect to the Universal life energy, which is the oneness in all life, flowing through you.

6. Accept your ability to give and receive the energy transfer.

Activating the Reiki Energy

1. Intent is paramount; whatever is positively requested will be activated.
2. Turn your hands up and ask for healing to come in.
3. Imagine a violet light entering your head first, then flowing into your heart and out your hands into the body of the receiver.
4. Wait until a sensation is felt, then apply it to the body.

Balancing Chakras

Because healing energy flows into the body through the seven major chakras, a good way to open a session is by balancing these chakras. When one begins by opening the chakras, the current of Reiki becomes much stronger. The locations of the chakras are not limited to the physical body. They extend out into the etheric body as well, so hold your hands above the body for this process.

There are three types of chakra balancing that can be used at the beginning of a session. These balances are also helpful during the Reiki 21- day cleanse when emotions are high or the mind cannot center. The *emotional balance* is done when the client feels emotionally ill-at-ease or off-center. The *intellectual balance* assists with mental clarity for work, school or creativity. The *quick chakra balance* is valuable when there is a time constraint.

Procedures to Balance the Chakras

The numbers for the chakras are shown in Chapter 4.

1. *Emotional Balance* - place hands on chakras 1 and 6.
   - One hand remains on chakra 1.
   - The hand at the head moves from chakra 6 down toward chakra 2, one chakra at a time.
   - Hold each position for 30 seconds to one minute or until there is an energy shift. It can happen in a matter of seconds.
2. *Intellectual Balance* - place hands on chakras 1 and 6.
   - The hand remains on chakra 6.
   - The other hand moves from chakra 1 up to chakra 5.
   - Move one chakra at a time, in the same manner as above.
3. *Quick Chakra Balance* - place hands on chakras 1 and 6.
   - Move hands in towards each other, holding chakras 2 and 5.
   - Complete by holding chakras 3 and 4.
   - These three hand placements will activate energy as follows:
     - For dyslexia - hold hands on chakras 1 and 6.
     - To express truth, hold hands on chakras 2 and 5.
     - To balance outer world knowledge with inner heart knowing, hold hands on chakras 3 and 4.

Grounding

While giving a treatment, the practitioner can feel off-centered, spacey and almost dizzy because there is so much energy entering the upper part of the body.

This is because Reiki flows through the head, heart and hands, which are all above the waist. When there is no attention given to move energy in the lower part of the body the practitioner can lose their center. To alleviate this problem, imagine opening the base chakra and allowing some of the Reiki to flow into the earth. Once received by Mother Earth, she responds by sending her nurturing energy back into the feet of the sender and through all the chakras. The practitioner can then direct the energy as guided. Opening and receiving earth love while pulling in Reiki from the sky creates a transfer of energy and becomes a two-way street.

Blend earth energy into the heart and through the hands while the remainder of light continues to flow up out of the head and descends over and into the aura in a rainbow of color. The colors hold a grounding essence, which will stabilize the body. It locks your feet to the ground like two magnets and you will feel very connected to the earth which makes a very solid sensation. The dizziness is immediately dispersed. It can be described as the sensation created when two magnets are held and then slowly brought together. First a resistance is felt and then an immediate pulling as they lock together. Notice if it feels the same when you send Reiki into the earth in the following "Life Tool."

 Life Tool: Grounding Cosmic Energy

1.	Before starting a treatment and upon its completion, it is important to ground the energy you have brought into the earth.
2.	As the cosmic energy enters your crown chakra and flows from your head into your heart, direct some of this light down to your base or first chakra.
3.	Intend for the chakras in your feet to open. Continue moving the energy into your legs and then out through the chakras in your feet.
4.	The cosmic light naturally descends to the center of the earth where it finds its way to a healing crystal.
5.	Wrap the cosmic energy around the crystal to deeply anchor the healing vibrations.
6.	Mother Earth will immediately respond by sending her nurturing love back through the same channels it came from.
7.	Invite the earth's healing love to flow up into your body through the channels of the chakras, in a rainbow of colors. Notice if the earth energy feels different than the Reiki light.
8.	The energy blends with the love in your heart and may be used for additional healing through your hands. Is there a new sensation?
9.	The rest of the earth frequency continues up and out of your crown and fountains down around your entire body.
10.	Within this colorful spray is a silver cord, which connects you to the essence of light high within the sky, while keeping you grounded deep within mother earth.
11.	Claim your power now and never again forget who and what you really are: a beautiful divine being of light.
12.	Your body is now fully grounded as it simultaneously channels earth and cosmic healing light. This is a very strong energy.

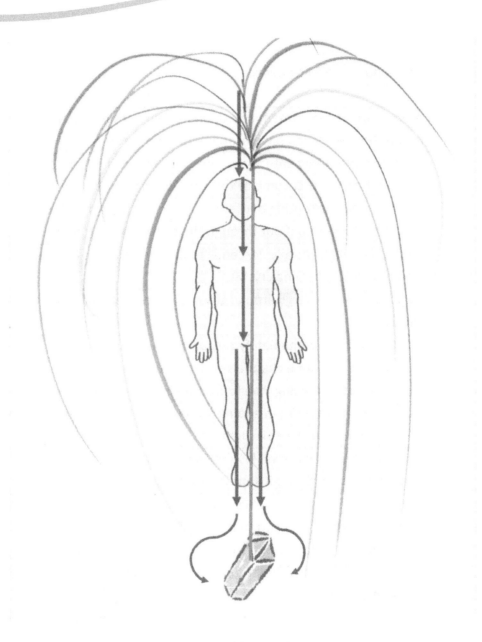

Flow of Cosmic and Earth Energies

Self-Treatment

To begin self-treatment:

1. Turn your palms upward.
2. Call in your Reiki energy and if you like, ask for help from your guides.
3. Ground yourself.
4. Accept your power and ability to give and receive Reiki.
5. State your intent for this healing session.
6. Draw the power symbol in front of your body.
7. Open and balance your chakras.
8. Hold each position for one minute. The 20 positions will complete a 20-minute Self-Reiki treatment.
9. Place your hands on your body and proceed with the following positions.
10. Verbally or mentally say the corresponding affirmations.

Positions:	Affirmations:
1. Hands over Eyes	"I am my clear sight. I see the beauty in myself and others."
2. Hands over Ears	"I am my intuitive hearing, receiving what people say from their hearts, not their voices."
3. Jaw line	"My teeth and gums are healthy. My jaw is relaxed."
4. Sides of Head	"The right and left sides of my brain are balanced." (Good for dyslexia).

5. Back of Head   "I am open to receiving the guidance of my Higher Self."

6. Neck and Throat   "I speak my truth kindly."

7. Throat and Heart   "Communication is open and guided by my heart."

8. Lower Rib Cage   "My organs are working in harmony. My blood is cleansed." (For gall bladder, spleen & liver).

9. Stomach and Intestines   "I can digest any situation that comes my way."

10. Groin   "I am secure in my sexuality."

11. Inside of Thighs   "My blood circulates freely throughout my body."

12. Knees   "I love myself. I am flexible and able to move forward easily."

13. Top and Base of Spine   "I am supported by life. I release all fear and blame."

14. Kidneys Adrenals   "I release disappointment, criticism, fear and and anger, then fill with joy and love"

15. Lower Back   "I am my infinite financial supply."

16. T-position (see page 66)   "I have all the support I desire."

17. Feet   "I am growing in my understanding of myself, life and others."

18. Inside of Feet   "I am growing in my understanding of myself, life and others."

Close your chakras

Ask for the chakras to be closed to the degree they need to be for that day. Place your hands over the top of your body, hands not touching the body, run your hands from the base chakra up to your nose, three times, thinking or stating a positive affirmation you have created for your day such as:

- I have a harmonious and healthy body.
- I am emotionally centered and joyous.
- I express confidence in my speech, actions and physical presence.

Seal yourself and ground

Draw the power symbol over your solar plexus for protection to ground and seal in the Reiki energy. The power symbol will be discussed in Chapter 3. The protection activated will slow down negative forces from entering your consciousness and energetic field. This is useful when out in public in crowded areas.

~ Remember to ground the energy,
for the healing energy will become stronger
when it is allowed to connect to the earth. ~

At the end of a session, imagine Reiki flowing from the head, through the heart, down through the base chakra and out the feet into the earth. Continue the direction of the healing energy deep into the core of the earth where there lies a healing crystal. Wrap your Reiki energy around the crystal and you will find Mother Earth responding. You can sense her love coming up into your feet. If not, pretend you do and it will stimulate your awareness so eventually you *will* physically feel it. The love continues through your entire body and out the top of your head in a colorful fountain. Within the fountain is a silver cord, which connects you to the Universal healing energy.

Give thanks to the guides, angels, and masters who have assisted. Ask for the Reiki to go out to bless and heal all living things on the planet, for the power of love, which is Reiki, is unlimited.

Self Healing Hand Positions

There is no reference to hand positions for specific ailments because Reiki is guided by a higher intelligence and travels to the place in the body or bodies - physical, mental, emotional or spiritual - where the love is most required. The affirmations aid in holding the intent to balance and state perfection for your body. Let the Universe fulfill the greatest need, relax and enjoy the energy.

Hands over Eyes

"I am my clear sight.
I see only beauty
in myself and others."

Hands over Ears

"I am my intuitive hearing,
receiving what people say
from their hearts, not their voices."

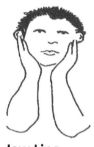

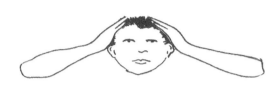

Jaw Line

Sides of Head

"My teeth and gums are
healthy. My jaw is relaxed."

"The right and left sides of
my brain are balanced."

Back of Head

Neck and Throat

"I am open to hearing the
guidance of my Higher Self."

"I speak my truth kindly."

Throat and Heart

"Communication is open
and guided by my heart."

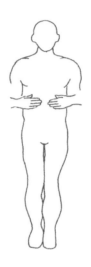

Lower Rib Cage

"My organs are working in harmony.
My blood is cleansed."

Stomach and Intestines

"I can digest any situation that
comes my way."

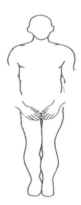

Groin

"I am secure in my
sexuality."

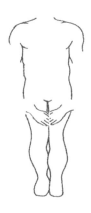

Inside Thighs

"My blood circulates freely
throughout my body."

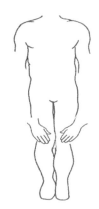

Knees

"I love myself. I am flexible and
able to move forward easily."

Top and Base of Spine

"I am supported by life;
I release all fear and blame."

Kidneys and Adrenals

"I release disappointment,
criticism, fear and anger,
then fill with joy and love."

 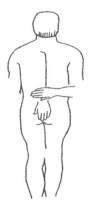

Lower Back

"I am my infinite financial supply."

T-Position

"I have all the support
I desire."

 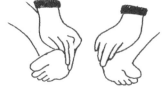

Feet

"I am growing in my understanding of myself, life and others."

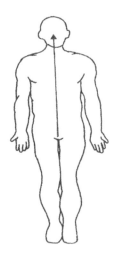

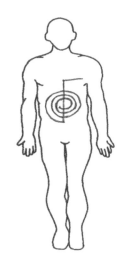

Close Chakras with a Positive Phrase

- I have a perfect healthy body.
- I am emotionally centered and joyous.
- I express confidence in my speech, actions and physical presence.

Seal and Ground
with
ChoKuRei

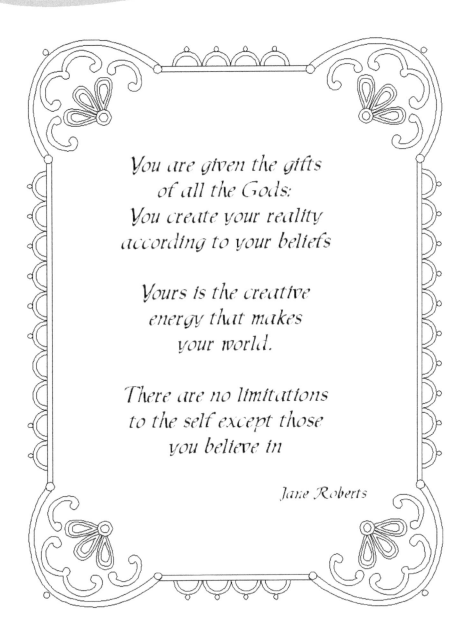

You are given the gifts
of all the Gods:
You create your reality
according to your beliefs

Yours is the creative
energy that makes
your world.

There are no limitations
to the self except those
you believe in

Jane Roberts

Chapter 3

The Symbols

Symbols have been used since the beginning of time to tell stories and to connect the physical to the divine. They are found throughout the world in petro glyphs in Utah, hieroglyphs in Egypt and carvings on caves in Tibet, just to name a few. There is a vibrational difference between the Reiki symbols and other geometric forms. Reiki symbols radiate the light from the higher self, which is a very high frequency. Other symbols receive their power from the conscious mind, the power we give it, thus these symbols may not be as potent.

Sacred Geometric Forms used throughout Societies

Reiki and its symbols raise the vibration of all the bodies of the individual: physical, mental, emotional and spiritual. The physical body is the only one that is visible; the others are unseen, yet easily sensed. Prove it to yourself. Notice that when another person stands too close, it feels uncomfortable. This is because your personal space has just been occupied without permission. This intruder has stepped into one of the three etheric bodies. There is no demarcation line to define this space, yet one is quite aware when another has crossed over this boundary. The invasion is within the spiritual, mental and emotional bodies. Reiki symbols increase the energy flow into these bodies by connecting to the universal energy, which flows around the body. In this way the body will receive healing in every aspect of its being, creating a lasting effect.

Symbols are activated by vibrations, which can be created through the sound of speaking the name of the symbol, by the act of drawing it or by simply holding the image in the mind. The movie *Contact* illustrates the concept of how sound, once put into the ethers, will never cease to exist. In the movie, the actress Jodie Foster plays a scientist who is fascinated with the exploration of contacting star systems as far away as humanly possible. She sends out signals and eventually receives back a signal of a 1940s newsreel broadcast. This is possible because radio and television frequencies are sound vibrations and once sent the vibrations of the sound do not stop; they continue into outer space for eternity.

Although *Contact* is a fictional story filmed in the 1990s, there is truth in their adaptation because there was an actual report of our astronauts receiving the sound of an old radio broadcast when they were traveling out in space. Every spoken word has a vibration; once spoken it continues to carry its intent forever. This is why avoiding detrimental words and speaking kindly is so important.

Radionics, a process which uses machines to access and adjust the subtle energy systems of items, can also measure the vibration of lines on paper, i.e. symbols. It has been seen when Reiki symbols are drawn or spoken, that their frequency and power are released. As with hands-on Reiki, the Reiki symbol emanates a very high, clear frequency and when drawn, it also emits vibration. It then seeks out its counterpart in the universe, which intensifies its power. Once the symbol is drawn, it brings in the healing energy of anyone who has ever used that symbol, thus tremendously empowering healing through the symbols.

Reiki symbols do not work through the subconscious or physical mind, as do religious forms. Reiki symbols connect to the higher self, thus moving beyond the limitations of the human mind and psyche. The symbol travels though space and time, much like prayer. There is no question as to its ability to be received by the higher self of the person toward which it is directed. A clear objective will manifest the required result.

After a period of practice, the symbols can be sent with only the designated objective. The practitioner acts as a clear channel, while the qualities of the symbols are activated through the mind when the thought for healing is sent. This is how the healer steps into their power and away from the dogma of the symbol. Nothing is stronger than the individual--not attunements, not symbols, not instruction. All of these assist the seeker, but the power is already there, just dormant. All of these activities are a reminder of what lies within and our ability to activate our power.

The way the symbols are drawn is not critical; it is the desire to assist another which gives them power. Translations have been made for the learning styles of different societies; therefore, to know your intent is most important. The guides understand the goal and follow the guidance of the higher self of the client. Once the energy flow is commissioned, the connection is made and the energy transfer will flow from higher self to higher self of the practitioner and client. The healer becomes a conduit of light and is blessed by the Universal love which is streaming through them.

The attunement received from the master teacher imprints the key of the symbol into the nervous system of the practitioner and activates the Reiki energy for the use of that symbol. The symbol does not have to be drawn perfectly to be recognized and activated by the spirit guides. Honor the symbol and draw it as accurately as possible, but do not become a perfectionist. Be clear in your mind as to what you want to accomplish and if it is of the highest good for the client, it will be granted.

All symbols were traditionally taught in the second level of Reiki. Because of the advancement of the planet and her people, many non-traditional masters are teaching the Power symbol in first degree of Reiki. I connected with my guides during the first year I was teaching and was also given permission to give this symbol to my students in first degree Reiki. I do not find it too advanced for the beginning student as they soon find how it seals a space in love, while it draws more Reiki power into any given situation.

The Power Symbol

Cho-Ku-Rei
  (Cho Koo Ray)

Japanese translation

Cho*:*   Curved sword
         Drawing a curved line

Ku: Penetrating
         To make a hole
         A place where there is nothing (ness)

Rei: Transcendent Spirit
         Mysterious power
         Essence

Drawing the symbol

1. The top line is drawn from right to left. This represents the flow of male energy.

2. The vertical line is drawn from top to bottom. This reflects energy flowing from above to the earth or down the spinal column.

3. The circle corresponds with female energy.

4. All of the lines come together to form a balanced whole.

5. Notice that the energetic flow crosses the spinal column seven times, to enhance each of the seven chakras.

Definition of Cho Ku Rei:

Drawing in the power of the Universe
Sealing a locale in light.

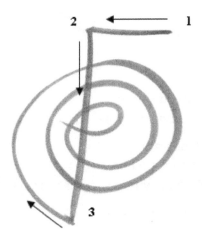

The Power Symbol
Cho Ku Rei

Practice Drawing Cho Ku Rei here ↑

Direct the laser beam from your hand chakra which is located in the center of your palm or out the tip of your middle finger, also called the *fire finger*. Channeling Reiki from this finger is more direct and penetrating.

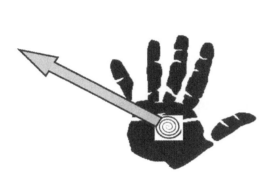

1. State the intent of how you want to use Cho-Ku-Rei.

2. Draw the symbol in the air.

3. Say the name of the symbol three times out loud if alone or silently if another is present.

4. Visualize a laser beam coming out of your hand chakra.

5. Reiki energy is violet. Therefore, you may imagine the symbol in violet light.

6. Before starting a treatment you may, but are not required to, draw the symbol on your hand chakra. This way you have a physical sensation of the symbol.

7. Picture the symbol in your mind and send it out with intent alone.

8. After scanning the body, place Cho-Ku-Rei over any area that calls for attention. This will quickly bring more energy to the area.

9. Draw a large Cho-Ku-Rei in the air in front of your body before starting and ending a healing treatment.

How to Use the Power Symbol

1. Cho-Ku-Rei is used to direct the energy of Reiki to one place.

2. Cho-Ku-Rei turns on Reiki energy and begins a direct flow.
    a. Like turning on a light switch, the power immediately comes through.
    b. Use it before starting to give Reiki.

3. Cho-Ku-Rei seals the energy.
    a. Use Cho-Ku-Rei at the end of a treatment, over the solar plexus.
    b. This seals and completes the treatment.
    c. A ring of golden energy is created around the client.
    d. Healing energy is contained so that it will not leak away.
    e. The benefit will be felt for hours or even days after the treatment.

4. During a treatment, after scanning the body, the practitioner will know where more power is needed.
    a. Draw the power symbol over those areas where guided.
    b. This increases the flow and the strength of the healing energy.
    c. The symbol breaks through blocks that may exist in those charged areas.

5. Draw the power symbol in front of your body.
    a. For protection.

    b. To empower yourself.

    c. To strengthen your aura.

6. Draw the power symbol over each chakra

    a. To clean and empower each one.

    b. As it is drawn, imagine each Cho-Ku-Rei the color of the corresponding chakra.

7. Apply the symbol when flying in a plane.

    a. Imagine the symbol at the door so that every traveler is calmed.

    b. See a Cho-Ku-Rei in the cockpit to align the pilots for a safe flight.

    c. Focus the energy of Cho-Ku-Rei on the wings and engines.

    d. Place one more symbol in each galley to bless the flight attendants.

    e. To still turbulence imagine a Cho-Ku-Rei over each wing and visualize the spiral extending below the wing. This will give the plane more mass so it will not rock in the wind.

8. Draw Cho-Ku-Rei on the bottoms of your feet.

    a. Then the feet are firmly anchored and grounded to the earth.

    b. Mother Earth will have an open channel to send her love back into the body of the sender, adding her peace to the cosmic love of Reiki.

9. To give a blessing to someone, visualize the power symbol on your palm as you shake their hand.

10. To protect and bless a room

    a. Visualize or draw Cho-Ku-Rei in all directions, including the ceiling and floor.

    b. Speak the name of the symbol three times.

    c. Say "I protect this room with light."

    d. Direct the energy to the center of the room and ground it to the earth.

    e. See the symbol empowering and filling the room with radiant energy.

    f. Use this wonderful tool before a treatment or meditation.

11. Goals
    a. Write the goal on a piece of paper.
    b. Visualize or draw the power symbol in living light over the goal.
    c. Send Reiki into the piece of paper while it is sandwiched between your hands.

12. Selling a House
    a. Draw the power symbol inside each room of the house with your hand or a smudge stick (dried wild sage wrapped with string.)
    b. Visualize or draw the power symbol in the yard; in the front back and sides.
    c. Place the power symbol on all advertisements and fliers.
    d. Imagine the power symbol over the real estate office, encompassing the agents.
    e. Visualize the perfect buyer surrounded with the symbols.
    f. Let go of the house and release how the sale should look while asking for the highest good for all involved.

13. Charging a dead car battery
    a. Raise the hood and draw the power symbol over the battery.
    b. Charge Reiki energy into the battery.
    c. Start the car.
    d. Reiki decreases the surface tension of water. This allows the chemicals in the battery to interact with the water, thus assisting the battery to work.
    e. This also works for cell phones; hold your hand over the phone and watch the battery bars move up.

14. Blessing food.
    a. Draw Cho-Ku-Rei over the prepared food or as you are cooking.
    b. This balances any negative energy from the cook or the server.
    c. Cho-Ku-Rei harmonizes the body to be more receptive to nutrients in the food.

  d. Your stomach will be able to relax and better digest your meal.

15. Blessing water.

  a. Look into your glass and imagine the power symbol in a glass of water.

  b. Draw Cho-Ku-Rei over the glass.

  c. Drinking the water at bedtime will improve and deepen sleep. You may have vivid and perhaps lucid dreams.

Chapter 4

The Chakras

Chakra is a Sanskrit word for *wheel*. They are energy vortices seen in the etheric body as wheels of light, flames or spinning circles. Traditionally, it is considered that we have seven major chakras and animals have them as well. Contemporary descriptions of the chakra system have been expanded to include an additional five more chakras. They are becoming activated and are a reflection of our continuing evolution. Therefore, our etheric bodies can be seen holding twelve major chakras. Not only are there chakras that attach to the body, but there are corresponding chakras in the auric field as well. But for simplicity we will be only addressing seven chakras in this level.

Chakras connect to the body at the spine and expand outside the physical body into the etheric body where they receive, transmit and process information. They are made up of vortices of energy, which emanate energy out and receive information in. Each chakra has a different number of vortices within it. The chakras, when fully open and functioning, span about six inches in

diameter and are perceived to be about one inch above the body. They draw energy in from the universal energy around us, somewhat like a whirlpool or gentle tornado. However, we are surrounded by more energy and information than we can possibly absorb. Therefore, our bodies regulate themselves by opening the chakras to draw in only the amount of information that can be absorbed at any given time. This is quite an amazing process.

David Tansley, author of *Radionics and the Subtle Bodies of Man*, describes the seven major chakras as places in the body where standing lines of light cross each other 21 times. Our bodies as well as the earth are intricate webs of light. We also have 21 minor chakras where the energy strands cross 14 times. As these energy lines cross, they begin to make up a light grid around the body. This grid can be seen by clairvoyants and is artistically diagrammed by Alex Grey in his book *Sacred Mirrors*. Many tiny vortices exist in the human body. These vortices are located at the junctures where numerous lines intersect. They often correspond to the acupuncture points of Chinese medicine. Many of the holistic healing modalities have information that crosses over, reflecting the oneness which exists in all living organisms and the similarities of medical and metaphysical teachings.

Our bodies receive energy and function by channeling the life force or light through the top of the head. It is then dispersed throughout the body. When this energy flows freely through the physical form, we experience physical health. Energetically, the light also enters the etheric body through the top of the head, but this time, when it is dispersed through our body, it is via the chakras. As the life force flows through the chakras, this energy influences us, both on an emotional and on a physical level.

When these energy centers or chakras are healthy, they freely allow the life force to enter the body. When they are blocked, physical discomfort or dis-ease can attack the body. As mentioned earlier, the definition of dis-ease is when the body is out of harmony and not at ease within itself. When a chiropractor adjusts the spine, they are opening a physical channel for the life force to flow through. Headaches can be caused by a misalignment of the vertebrae in the spine. When the doctor aligns the vertebrae, the energy is dislodged and begins to flow smoothly as the pain ceases. Blockage in the chakras can also cause discomfort and can be opened by intent with hand positions on specific areas of the body.

The chakras assist the body with distributing energy through the physical, mental, emotional, and spiritual bodies. This results in an integrated holistic system: the body, mind, and spirit. Chakras are open and fully functioning at conception, but they close down and redevelop as the body grows from the womb to twenty-one years of age. The process never stops and the development continues throughout life. Cyndy Dale author of *New Chakra Healing* goes into detail how this amazing process affects us until well into our 80s.

When a trauma occurs during a developmental stage of life, the physical body will respond. As adults we are aware of where we hold stress. When agitated, one may encounter migraine headaches, digestive upsets, bronchitis or sinus problems. Each of these ailments encompasses a specific part of the body, which has a corresponding chakra in that locale. The time frame when a trauma has occurred is very often during the same time when this chakra was developing. This information alone may assist in clearing old ailments and the emotional attachment to them.

The past disturbance may appear non-threatening to an adult, but to a child it can be catastrophic and the body will react in turn. These issues are hidden, because when we look back at our childhood we are seeing it from an adult perspective and they do not seem as insurmountable as they did when we were small.

Example: To uncover the truth, imagine yourself three feet tall, looking up at everyone and everything around you. See your parents as your Gods. They have given you life and they keep you alive with warmth, protection and love in the way they know how. By holding our parents in this divine light, when they act inappropriately, it becomes devastating to a child.

Trauma can come in many forms. Ones that seem to be uneventful to an adult can be very disturbing to a young child. The obvious issues of death of a family member, sexual abuse and physical abuse are not the only situations that cause the chakra to under-develop. The birth of a sibling can be disturbing because it appears to diminish the time and love a child formerly received solely from their mother. Financial stress in the home, divorce or separation of the parents or simply moving to a new home can also disrupt the young child's world.

To see how this applies to your personal ailments, look at the following chakra chart later, it designates the time each chakra has developed. First, recall how your body reacts to stress. Do you get headaches, stomach disorders, colds, bronchitis or sinus problems? Find which chakra corresponds. Headaches are chakra six or seven; stomach is chakra number two, colds are chakra four and sinus is chakra six. Now find the age when this chakra was developing and recall what was going on in your life at that time that could have been upsetting to you as a young child.

Chakra Chart

Name of Chakra	Root Base	Sacral Spleen	Solar Plexus	Heart	Throat	Third Eye Brow	Crown
Number	1	2	3	4	5	6	7
Color	Red	Orange	Yellow	Green	Blue	Indigo	Violet or White
Foods	Proteins Beans Nuts	Water Juice Tea	Complex Carbs. Starches Grains	Green Veggies Dark Leafy Vegetables	Raw Fruits Blue & Purple Fruits +Veggies	Chlorophyll Breath Air	Fasting Juice Sun
Music Sounds	C O LAM	D Ooo VAM	E AHH RAM	F AY YAM	G EE HAM	A OM MMM	B NNN Silence
Crystals Stones	Garnet, Pyrite Bloodstone Hematite, Ruby	Coral, Citrine Moonstone Carnelian Fire Opal	Amber Tiger Eye Golden Topaz Citrine	Emerald, Jade Fluorite Aventurine Chrysocolla	Lapis, Sodalite Sapphire Turquoise Aquamarine	Amethysts Purple Fluorite Iolite Clear Quartz	Diamond Selenite Kunzite, Gold
Element	Earth	Water	Fire	Air	Ether	Thought	Light
Endocrine Glands	Ovaries Gonads	Liver Pancreas	Adrenal Glands	Thymus Gland	Thyroid Gland	Pituitary Gland	Pineal Gland
Age	Womb to 6 months	6 months to 2 ½ years	2 ½ years to 4 ½ years	4 ½ years to 6 ½ years	6 ½ years to 8 ½ years	8 ½ years to 14 years	14 years to 21 years

Emotions affect the body; once the origin is uncovered, the issue can be cleared. Energy healing sessions can harbor a safe space and a feeling of love, so the client can process and understand the underlying cause of dis-ease in the body. Once the cause is discovered, hands-on healing will transmit love into the body and greatly aid in releasing emotional and physical pain. Reiki also softens and opens the heart so the incidents can be revealed in a caring light. Many of the answers lie within the chakras. Using guided imagery will reveal to the client the basis of their distress. The beauty of Reiki is that the higher self is directing the healing to where it needs to be, even when the issue is not verbally addressed. Eventually the real reason for the distress will be presented to the client by their higher self as a new awareness surfaces. This may happen in a way totally unknown by the practitioner but the practitioner is the one who opened the energy so this may occur.

"Life Tools" are found throughout the book and are guided imagery meditations, which open the psyche and clear the illusion that was once held in the body. An old issue can be seen in a new light and old perceptions released. The following "Life Tool: Chakra Opening" is designed to allow one to get in touch with the energetic essence of the body via the chakras.

7 Crown
Connection to the Divine

#6 Third Eye
Intuitive Abilities

5 Throat
Expression on all Levels

#4 Heart
Giving and Receiving
Love and Balance

#3 Solar Plexus
Seat of Emotions

#2 Sacral
Creativity and Passion

#1 Base
Opening to earthly gifts
and grounding

Hands and Feet are secondary
chakras to the Heart

Chakras are the lens from which
we observe the world through our
body.

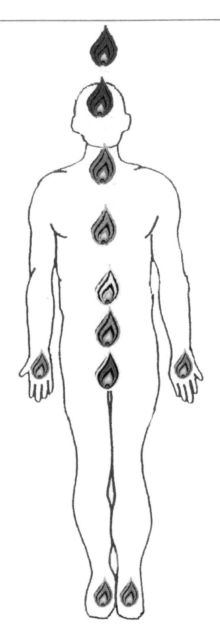

 Life Tool: Chakra Opening

1. Begin by stilling your body and releasing tension by taking three slow, deep breaths.
2. Pretend your <u>crown chakra</u> is opening and an iridescent light is entering in.
3. Allow the light to flow down into your <u>third eye</u>, at the forehead.
4. The color is indigo, a beautiful violet blue color.
5. Allow this light to radiate out of your forehead like a searchlight.
6. Assume this light can illuminate the direction you need to acquire everything your heart desires.
7. Let this light then flow into your <u>throat</u>, where it blends with a blue light.
8. Take a moment to connect to the power that is held in the spoken word.
9. The blue light vibrates into your words, making them clear and precise, along with your inner truth.
10. Imagine this power entering a green light in your <u>heart chakra</u>; it fills your entire chest cavity. Feel the balance, the love and the flow.
11. Sense the love entering into your heart as you breathe in and allow the love to move out as you exhale. This is a natural flow. Relax with it and notice any activity in your body as peace radiates from your heart and encompasses the physical form.
12. Open your heart and allow the love to flow into the emotional center of your <u>solar plexus</u>. It is golden yellow in color.
13. Feel the warmth it creates, calming the nervous system. Honor every emotion contained within this center; deny or judge none.
14. Sense the joy, the tears, the anger or the fear.

15.	Give each emotion the space to be expressed without judgment and be present with your feelings in this exact moment.
16.	Direct your energy lower in your body and open your <u>sacral chakra</u>. Move this balanced emotion into the area below the navel, which is a glowing orange color. The color lights up a dark corner in your imagination as you become aware of and honor your creative self.
17.	Allow the light to enter this chakra as new ideas begin to form.
18.	Let creativity flow into your <u>root chakra</u>. It is a brilliant red, full of possibilities; it anchors and grounds to Mother Earth.
19.	Open this chakra and feel the energy flowing in like a gentle breeze. This breeze brings in an unlimited supply of everything physical, all that your heart can imagine.
20.	Continue flowing energy through all of your chakras down deep into the center of the earth to anchor and ground your new perceptions.
21.	The rainbow colors of your chakras find their way to the core of the earth, where a healing crystal lies. Wrap the colors around the crystal and connect to the love of Mother Earth.
22.	Once this connection is made it will flow back to your body, entering all the chakras, until the light of the earth exits out the top of your head in a beautiful colorful fountain. It will then flow down across your entire body.
23.	Anchoring to the earth is now possible, as your body is grounded deep within the core of mother earth while simultaneously connected to all that "is" in the universe.
24.	When you feel complete, take a deep breath, open your eyes and feel completely refreshed.

Qualities of Chakras

1st - Root or Base Chakra

Represents:

This is the first chakra to develop in the womb. It holds our basic existence. Here lie our primary needs such as water, food, shelter, sex, love/being loved, survival, basic tribal (family) programming, will or right to survive, passion, will to live, ability to stand up for one's self, ability to provide for life's necessities, the center for life-promoting energy and grounding.

Stones that resonate with this chakra:

Ruby, red garnet, red jasper, pyrite, rhodochrosite, smoky quartz, black tourmaline, tourmalinated quartz.

2nd - Sacral or Spleen Chakra

Represents:

Anchored in this center most of all is our creativity. The procreation of life comes from this area of the body: women through the ovaries, men through their sperm. Therefore, it is the place where most women store their life energy. This is the center of sensation and emotion, consciousness of creativity, control of most personality functions, giving and receiving, sexual passion and love, relationship with money, power and control, ethics and honor in relationships and blame and guilt.

Stones that support this chakra:

Amber, citrine, coral, gold peridot, tiger eye, gold topaz, peach aventurine.

3rd - Solar Plexus Chakra

Represents:
Personal power, will, trust, linked to rational thought process, self-esteem, self-confidence and self-respect, sensitivity to criticism, personal honor, responsibility for making decisions and the source of men's power.

Stones that support this chakra:
Amber, aquamarine, emerald, malachite, peridot, pyrite, smoky quartz, tiger eye, rutilated quartz, citrine.

4th - Heart Chakra

Represents:
Divine and unconditional love, resentment and bitterness, love and hatred, self-centeredness, forgiveness, compassion, balance and peace through a yin yang effect. Being the center chakra it holds a balance between the earth and the sky. There is also a secondary chakra located in the palm of each hand and the center of each foot, which connects directly to the heart.

Stones that support this chakra:
Jade, rose quartz, ruby, green fluorite, bloodstone, red garnet, gold, moonstone, rhodochrosite, red or pink tourmaline.

5th - Throat Chakra

Represents:
Power of how we express ourselves, the spoken word, how we communicate our creativity and thoughts, strength of our will, addictions, judgment and criticism, using personal power to create, capacity to make decisions, following one's dream, self-protection, the seat of responsibility (the ability to say yes or no.)

Stones that support this chakra:
Aquamarine, lapis lazuli, sapphire, blue topaz, turquoise.

6th - Brow or Third Eye Chakra

Represents:
Clairvoyance, concentration, magnetic attraction of towards the feminine aspects of our energies, openness to the ideas of others, ability to learn from experience and self-evaluation.

Stones that support this chakra:
Amethyst, azurite, kyanite, lapis lazuli, moldavite, sapphire, sodalite, sugilite, blue topaz, blue tourmaline.

7th - Crown Chakra

Represents:
Our spiritual essence, our connection to the Universal energy and our higher-self, integration of our spiritual self with our physical self, perception beyond space and time, ability to trust life, faith and inspiration, values, ethics and courage.

Stones that support this chakra:
Alexandrite, amber, amethyst, citrine, diamond, gold, clear quartz crystal, rutilated quartz, selenite, sugilite, gold topaz, tourmalinated quartz, zircon.

Chapter 5

The Treatment

Before a treatment, it will be beneficial in the beginning to spend time preparing your personal self on all levels and in all four bodies. Address the spiritual body by lighting a candle, burning incense or placing your attention on a master of healing. Healing masters can be Jesus for love, Quan Yin for compassion, St. Germaine for clearing, Buddha for oneness or any great being towards whom you feel an affinity. If you are going to burn incense, do it a few hours before the arrival of the client. This way, if they are sensitive to fragrances, they will not be offended. It is the energy and intent of burning incense that gives its clearing power; the scent is only part of the focus.

The mental body will quiet when you meditate for five to ten minutes, while holding a clear intent to assist the client in any way necessary. Turn off all

phones, including cell phones and pagers. This will assure that your mental body will not be jarred by inconvenient calls. Clear your mind and release worry and concern about upcoming schedules or duties. While in the stillness of your mind, imagine connecting to the higher self of the client. Ask what needs to be done. An intuitive message need not be picked up for the connection to be made as it will happen automatically. The call compels the answer. You will be directed on the inner planes and the treatment will be divinely directed. The key is to trust and to know that you are guided by the highest source of yourself and the client.

The emotional body becomes quiet when it is connected to the heart. As Universal light is channeled into the body, the heart will automatically open and at that point, the emotions will still. Meditation before a session will attend to the activation of this calm interface. If the intent is made for love to fill the emotions, the process will be granted.

The physical body can come into alignment by taking a short walk, even if it is just a few steps onto the grass around the location where the treatment is given. This will ground you to mother earth and bring in her loving, healing light. If time permits, a longer walk gives time to still the mind, connect with nature, clear the lungs and release the hustle of the day or the expectation for a specific result from the treatment.

Instruct the client about how Reiki could feel to their body. They may feel warmth, tingling or energy surges, and emotions could arise. If they fall asleep, it does not diminish the treatment. The body takes what it needs; if it requires rest, it will sleep. The unconscious mind rules the conscious mind. Often when sleep occurs during the treatment, the client is actually moving their conscious mind out of the way so that the healing may flow into the unconscious, where lasting changes occur.

Have available a glass of water for when the client arrives and pour one for yourself as well. During a treatment, as a practitioner you may feel a tickle in your throat. It can become disturbing during a session when the energy is still and a cough begins to arise. It could be your own issue or you could be clearing energy for the client through your own body. A sip of water will often quiet this uneasy feeling. For the comfort of the client, offer to place a light blanket over their body, because when the body begins to make energetic changes, it often drops in temperature. Offer the water to your client at the end of the treatment to assist in bringing them back to this world and grounding them so they are steady on their feet when they leave.

The first five or ten minutes of the treatment should take the form of an intake interview. Ask the client what they would like to address in this session on all levels: physical ailments, personal relationships or business and employment concerns. This will bring to the surface the issues the client wants to clear. Sometimes they may retrieve information they were not previously aware of just by being in the presence of the Reiki energy, via the practitioner. Reiki works with the unconscious mine through the divine self of the client, but there is also a conscious side which also needs be honored. Once the conscious mind is appeased by giving it its say, it will still and the unconscious will arise to be healed. The process works on many levels, often beyond the understanding of the mind. Be clear on the intent to help and positive changes will occur.

The hands-on healing treatment will open the brow chakra, where intuitive messages may be obtained by both the client and the practitioner. The client may access this, in the quiet time during the one hour treatment or they may become aware of new insights later, usually within three days after the treatment; so tell them to be observant of their thoughts for the next few days. The early hours of the morning are particularly receptive to spiritual guidance.

During the session, ask the client to concentrate on a question they would like to have guidance on and offer it up to their higher self and then be open to receive an answer. The response may come in a dream, an image, in a song on the radio, on a billboard or during a conversation with another person. If they are watchful they can receive guidance during everyday activities. They become their own detective, uncovering information that will be revealed in interesting and often humorous ways. By this instruction you are helping your client to pick

up on their natural intuitive skills. Reiki is not only about healing it is about teaching others how they can do their own self healing.

Preparation before Giving a Treatment

1. Inform client you are not a massage therapist and therefore not licensed to manipulate the body. Reiki works in the four energy fields of the body: physical, mental, emotional and spiritual. Therefore, it clears at a very deep level without physical body manipulation.
2. If the client is not familiar with Reiki, spend ten minutes explaining how Reiki works and how it may affect them during the following days. Explain that during the treatment they may experience
   a. Tingling or warmth.
   b. Energy surges.
   c. Deep relaxation and peace.
   d. Sleepiness.
   e. Emotions.
   f. Nothing at all.
   g. Sensations that vary with each treatment and with each person.
3. Spend a few minutes at the start to find out the reason for their session.
4. Fill out a "Progress and Treatment Report" to keep track of results.
5. Offer a glass of water to your client and have one available for yourself.
6. Place a blanket over the client for comfort, if desired.
7. Ask your client if there is a question they would like to ask their higher self.
8. Have them concentrate on the question during the treatment.
9. Let them know the answer will come during the treatment or within the next few days. This happens because their crown chakra will open during

the treatment which will allow for clear information to come through from their higher self.

10. Remind the client that, even if they feel nothing at all, the energy has entered their body and change is inevitable. Tell them to watch for it.

Treatment with Hands off the Body

When the hands are off the body of the client, one is working directly on the aura. The aura is where dis-ease originates. When emotional problems are ignored or stuffed away, they are sustained in the aura around the body. If they go unattended and ignored for an extended period of time, the original cause becomes hidden and buried. Then these issues have time to build in power and when manifested in the physical body, they are seen as diseases or ailments. Reiki works with all four bodies: physical, mental, emotional and spiritual. Thus, it can bring to the surface the core issue. When energy work is used on a regular basis, it acts as preventative medicine to clear the body of deep-seated emotional problems, because it addresses issues in all these bodies.

Traditional Reiki is a practice which is done with the hands directly on the body. The belief in traditional Reiki is that when the hands are off the body, Reiki ceases; energy is transferred but it is not Reiki. Reiki is channeling Universal light into the physical form; the non-traditional approach affirms that Reiki flows even when the hands are lifted from the body. To give a complete treatment with your hands entirely off the body can be tiring and unnecessary. During the session the hands are lifted from the body when intuitively guided and while doing a clearing at the end of the treatment. Working off the body at the end of the treatment will lift and clear anything that has been brought up for release during the treatment that can be moved out of the aura. This greatly aids the client and has a calming effect.

Clearing through the aura at the end of a treatment will also release issues in the spiritual, mental and emotional bodies. Place your hands about three feet

above the body, which is about one arm's length. As you bring your hands down through the aura, be aware of any heavy areas where the energy seems to be stuck. Swirl or move this energy to clear it away. The aura encompasses the entire body, so there is no need to clear both the head and the feet. One sweep will clear that layer completely around the body. Be careful not to draw the energy toward yourself. Just brush it out and away.

Re-check the aura again by starting three feet above the body and moving down through the aura. You will be surprised at how fast the auric energy field can be cleared. The process will only take a few minutes.

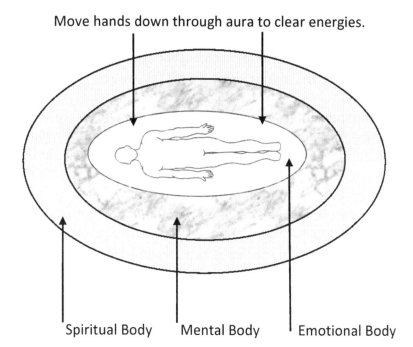

Move hands down through aura to clear energies.

Spiritual Body   Mental Body   Emotional Body

Scanning allows the practitioner to intuitively read, through sensations in their hands, what is happening in the client's body. When the practitioner glides one or both hands across the body about three inches above the client's body, deviations in energy flow can be felt. The practitioner is looking for any *differences* between the body areas. The specific sensation felt is not of primary importance here.

Example: It does not matter whether the body feels hot or cold. What matters is how one area is sensed *compared* to the rest of the body. The healer is picking up information from the bodies energy field. These differences mean this part of the body is calling for attention. This helps the healer to know where to spend more time during the session.

The Reiki attunement heightens the students' sensitivity and increases intuition. With practice you will experience the different sensations as your intuition becomes clearer. When you access information intuitively about the client it is not always necessary to mention it especially if the client has not brought it to your attention. Some traumatic experiences have been so deeply buried; the client may not have uncovered them yet. It is in their energy field which is why you may pick up the information. When they are ready to face an old issue, it will surface for them to see. Sometimes we as healers are privy to information which has not surfaced for the client and it is for our eyes only. In this way the practitioner can direct energy to the event without further trauma to the client. When the client is strong enough, the issue will arise and with Reiki treatments, they will be supported to receive and understand the reasons for the disturbing incident.

As you scan the body you may want to share with your client what you are detecting in their physical body. Perhaps there might be warmth over a knee or wrist which would show a need is this area. It could be an old injury or a chronic

ailment. There are two benefits from this process. It builds confidence in you and your client for you. When they affirm there is or was a problem in this area they relax and know they are in good intuitive hands. You are then encouraged to continue to express what is sensed as it builds your self confidence and self esteem.

Don't fret, for you can never be wrong. Even if there is not physical ailment in that area of the body at this time that does not negate your intuition. Reiki is preventive medicine. It works in the etheric bodies before the issue will manifest into the physical body. When an area is in need you may be clearing the etheric body with Reiki thus eliminating the need for dis-ease later in the body. Tell your client that their body is calling for the Reiki in this area to prevent a future physical disturbance.

How to Scan

1. Before beginning a treatment, ask your guides to show you where Reiki is required in the body.
2. Place your hand one to four inches above the body.
   a. You *may* feel: coolness, warmth, tingling, pressure or a magnetic pulling of your hand toward the body.
   b. These sensations indicate that you are detecting a need in that area of the body.
3. Trust your intuition. Do not think that what you feel is your imagination.
4. Share with your client what you are physically sensing.
5. You may become aware of the cause of an energy disturbance.
6. In this case:
   a. Only share information with your client when you are guided to do so.
   b. Share constructive information such as colors or feelings, not disturbing images.

    c. Get feedback from the client. You may be surprised to hear what your client sees.

7. After scanning, use the Reiki power symbol over any areas where energetic differences were detected. This will cause a greater intensity of healing energy to be absorbed by these areas during the session.

Self-Scanning

1. Use the same process as above.
2. Ask for guidance from your higher self to assist in understanding how the disorder was created.
3. Accept what is shown without judgment.
4. Often we are too critical of ourselves.
    a. Accept that the issues can be opportunities to grow, thus raising our consciousness to become a more illuminated healer.
    b. Be ready to forgive yourself and others and to let love in.

Beaming

When using this technique, the practitioner will be standing outside the etheric bodies of the client, channeling in the energy. A difference can be felt between how the energy is flowing through the practitioner's body and how the energy is coming from their hands.

For this process, the practitioner will hold their hands off of the client's body while standing outside of the client's aura. This will be about three feet away from their body. The area to be treated is in the aura itself, the place where disease starts in the body. Usually the energy is not directed at any specific location in the client. When one stands outside of the client's aura, the energy delivered is much clearer and unobstructed by the energy of the practitioner. The client is

not in the energy field of the practitioner and the practitioner is not in theirs. This allows the purest form of Reiki to flow without compromise from the personal energy of the practitioner.

Beaming is best done at the end of a treatment. To the practitioner's hands, beaming feels as though the client is a magnet drawing the energy into them. The drawing of the energy can really be felt in the practitioner's hands. Ask the client how this process feels different from the hands-on treatment. Most people will feel a contrast from earlier in the session when hands were directly on them. Some clients feel waves of pulsing energy, others feel warm all over and some feel no difference at all. It does not matter what is sensed or not, Reiki always works, 100% of the time. It works on all levels, conscious, subconscious, physical, mental, emotional and spiritual.

To charge energy into an individual area while not touching the body, the practitioner may see the energy coming out of the chakras of their hands and going to the area of need. It may also simply be directed with the eyes. Because the aura enfolds the entire body, the light will flow throughout the entire body even without direction.

Your intent gives Reiki more power. As you keep your attention on the healing you wish to render, your energy will be focused and will strengthen the flow of energy to that space. When you ask Reiki to flow, it will flow no matter where your thoughts may be. Remember, however, that when your attention is on the Reiki, the light will be stronger as it flows to its destination.

As outside thoughts come in, just sweep them away. Bring your attention back to your original purpose, *healing with the Universal life force.* Even when your mind wonders, which it will, the Reiki is still being transmitted. You are a channel for the energy; you are not using your own chi for the treatment and that is why you are never drained of your own energy.

Before Starting:

1. Call in your Reiki energy.
2. Turn your palms upward and sense the healing energy entering in.
3. Accept your power and ability to give and receive Reiki.
4. Ground yourself and enfold yourself in a bubble of pure light.
5. See the energy of your own chakras flowing down your legs, through the chakras in your feet, creating a grounding cord to the center of the earth.
6. Bring the healing energy of Mother Earth up this grounding cord, through all your chakras, until it exits out the top of your head in a fountain.
7. State the intent for this healing session or ask for the highest good of all.

To Begin:

1. When the client is resting on the massage table, stand at their head and draw the power symbol in front of your body.
2. Place your hands on the client's chest and yours to connect heart to heart.
3. Take a moment to call in any additional assistance by using your own personal affirmations or visualizations.
4. Scan the client's body and note where the areas are and give more attention to those locations.
5. Balance the chakras with:
    a. an emotional balance
    b. an intellectual balance or
    c. a quick balance
6. Hold each hand position for three minutes. The 20 hand positions, when completed, will fill a one-hour Reiki session.

Hand Positions for Others

Allow Reiki to flow from your hands into the client, in each of the following hand positions. You always have the freedom to move your hands to a more comfortable position when called upon. State the affirmations out loud or repeat them silently for inner focus and direction. Client is on the massage table, facing up, with a small pillow under their head and another under their knees for back comfort.

	Positions	**Affirmations**
1.	Hands over Eyes	"I am my clear sight. I see the beauty in myself and in others."
2.	Hands over Ears	"I am my intuitive hearing, receiving what people say from their hearts, not their voices."
3.	Jaw Line	"My teeth and gums are healthy. My jaw is relaxed."
4.	Sides of Head	"The right and left sides of my brain are balanced." (Good for dyslexia.)
5.	Back of Head	"I am open to receiving the guidance of my higher self."
6.	Shoulders	"All tension is released from my body."
7.	Neck and Throat	"I speak my truth kindly."
8.	Throat and Heart	"Communication is open and guided by my heart."
9.	Lower Rib Cage	"My organs are working in harmony. My blood is cleansed." (For gall bladder, spleen & liver)

10. Stomach and   "I can digest any situation that
    Intestines   comes my way."

11. Arms   "I freely give and receive with my heart."

While standing at the shoulders, face your client's feet. Sandwich one of your client's arms between your hands and arms. Place your outside arm under the client's arm and your inside arm on top of the client's arm. Repeat for the client's other arm.

12. Groin   "I am secure in my sexuality."

13. Inside of Thighs "My blood circulates freely
                         throughout my body."

14. Knees   "I love myself. I am flexible and able to
                         move forward easily."

15. Feet   "My Chi flows from head to toe."

Place your fingertips at the base of the client's toes and press firmly into the pads below the toes. This opens the energy along the Chinese medicine meridian lines.

Ask client to turn over and face down; move the pillow from their knees to under their ankles, the pillow under the head may be removed if it is more comfortable for the client.

16. Spine   "I am supported by life and I release all
                         fear and blame, then fill with love and joy."
Place your hands over the spine and continue with hand positions down to the base of the spine.

17. Kidneys   "I release disappointment, criticism, fear
    and Adrenals   and anger."

18. T-position   "I have all the support I desire."

19. Inside of Thighs "My blood circulates with ease
                         throughout my body."

20. Back of Knees   "I love myself. I am flexible and able to move forward easily."

21. Feet   Sandwich one of the client's feet between your hands, then the opposite foot.

22. Inside of Feet   "I am growing in my understanding of life, myself and others."

Closing

1. Ask client to turn over and face up.

2. Silently ask for their chakras to be closed to where they need to be for the day.

3. Turn your left palm upwards to receive divine light.

4. Above the body, move your right hand from the base chakra up to the nose while silently stating a positive affirmation for health such as:
   "I am perfect just the way I am."
   "I am emotionally sound and happy."

5. Repeat all of #4 three times.

6. Aura Clearing:
   a. Check the auric layers by running your hands down through the aura.
   b. Move any energy blocks out as needed.
   c. Smooth out the aura with your hands.

7. Seal in the client's energy by drawing the power symbol over their solar plexus.

8. Express gratitude and thanks for the healing received.

9. Ground yourself and the client.

10. See the energy of your own chakras flowing down your legs, through the chakras in your feet, creating a grounding cord to the center of the earth.

11. Bring the healing energy of Mother Earth up this grounding cord, through all your chakras, until it exits out the top of your head like a fountain, within it a *silver cord*.

12. See this silver cord extending from the top of your head to your higher self, the physical sun and beyond. This is where you receive your power from: deep within the earth and high within the sky.

13. Now proceed to visualize similar cords extending from your client as well.

After the Session

1. Have your client sit up. Offer them a glass of water and drink one yourself to further ground both of you.

2. Hand your client their shoes so they do not bend over and possibly become dizzy.

3. Ask for feedback from the client and note their responses in the "Client Record Form" which is found at the end of Chapter 6.

4. Offer any comments or educational information you feel could be helpful.

5. Give the client the "What is a Reiki Treatment" form found in Chapter 6.

6. Point out:
   a. The need for eight glasses of water a day to flush out toxins.
   b. Their body may experience a three-day cleanse, which can be physical, mental, spiritual, or emotional.
   c. Reiki is subtle; therefore, the benefits may be missed if one does know where to look and does not stay aware.

7. After your client has left, wash your hands and arms (up to elbows) in cold water to release energies.

8. Take a moment to meditate.

9. Sit in your Reiki room for five or ten minutes, while doing Reiki on yourself and absorbing the healing energy previously released.

10. Send the Reiki energy into the Universe to bless all life.

Hand Positons for Healing Others

Reiki flows to the part of the body where there is the greatest need. Therefore, there are no references to hand positions for specific ailments. Reiki is guided by a higher intelligence and travels into all the bodies, physical, mental, emotional or spiritual, thus addressing issues before they manifest in the physical body in forms of dis-ease. The affirmations aid in holding the intent to balance and state perfection for the body and may be spoken audibly or in the silence of your mind.

Let go of the expectations of what the treatment needs to accomplish and place your trust in the Universe. The greatest good will be fulfilled, so relax and enjoy the energy for when you give Reiki you too are receiving its' balancing love.

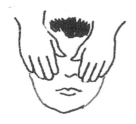

Hands over Eyes

"I am my clear sight.
I see the beauty in
myself and others."

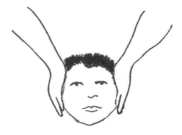

Hands over Ears

"I am my intuitive hearing;
receiving what people say from
their hearts, not their voices."

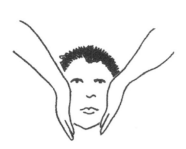

Jaw Line
"My teeth and gums are healthy.
My jaw is relaxed."

Sides of Head
"The right and left sides of
my brain are balanced."

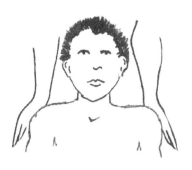

Back of Head

"I am open to receiving the
guidance of my Higher Self."

Shoulders

"All tension is released
from my body."

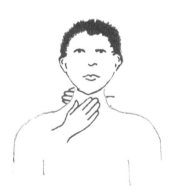

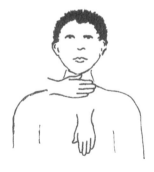

Neck and Throat

"I speak my truth kindly."

Throat and Heart

"Communication is open
and guided by my heart."

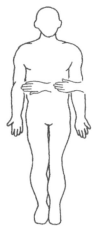

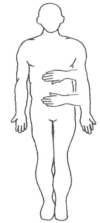

Lower Rib Cage

"My organs are working in harmony. My blood is cleansed."

Stomach and Intestines

"I can digest any situation that comes my way."

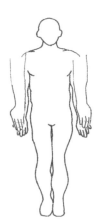

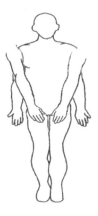

Arms
"I freely give and receive with my heart."

Groin
"I am secure in my sexuality."

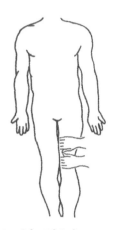

Inside Thighs

"My blood circulates freetly
throughout my body."

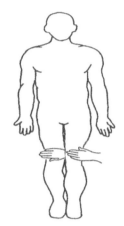

Knees

"I love myself. I am flexible and
able to move forward easily."

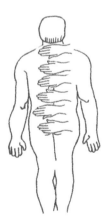

Spine
"I am supported by life;
I release all fear and blame."

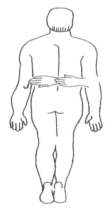

Kidneys and Adrenals
"I release disappointment,
fear and anger then fill with
love and joy."

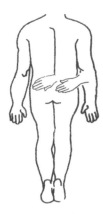

Lower Back

"I am my infinite financial supply."

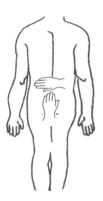

T-Position

"I have all the support
I desire.

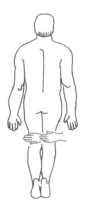

Back of Knees

"I love myself and am
able to move forward easily."

Feet

"I am growing in my understanding
of myself, life and others."

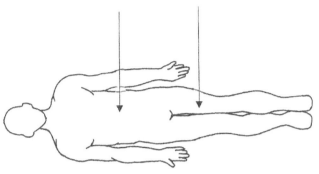

Complete the process and clear aura by moving your hands down through the clients etheric bodies. Notice any resistance and sweep the stagnant energy out and away from you.

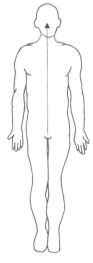

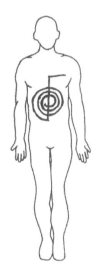

Ask for the chakras to be adjusted as needed. Either open or slightly closed and then give a positive personal affirmation for the client.

Seal and Ground
with
Cho Ku Rei

- I have a harmonious and healthy body
- I am emotionally centered and joyous
- I express confidence in my speech, actions and physical presence.

Children mimic our habits, the good ones along with the bad. When they see a loved one giving and receiving the light of Reiki they naturally want to do the same. When their curiosity is supported they will naturally blossom. More than one of my students have shared how their children, less than five years old, automatically begin to give Reiki in return when it is administered to them. They need no attunement to transfer this healing because they are just using their natural abilities. When you honor and encourage them to use these instinctive tendencies on themselves and others, you will assist them in becoming confident self-assured adults.

There is little need to use lengthy hand positions when giving children Reiki as they respond very quickly to the energy and usually do not require full hour session. Hold the child or baby in your arms and think of Reiki flowing from your higher self, into your crown, through your heart and out your hands into their tiny body. When a baby turns away after you have given them only a few minutes of Reiki, know the session is complete. Their small bodies absorb the energy and distribute it to the appropriate area very quickly. They require no more attention until the next time you sense a need.

An easy way to calm an active child before bed is to place them on your lap while reading them a story and imagine Reiki raining over them. Their energy becomes still as their eye lids begin to close. I use this technique with my granddaughter and I find she wants to hear the end of the story but as soon as the last page is turned she will lie down, turn over and close her eyes.

Example: Years ago my youngest child was crying one night just before bedtime with a painful headache. I placed my hands on her head and within a few minutes she slowly placed her head upon the pillow and fell quickly asleep. Just try Reiki on these little ones before you reach for an aspirin and notice the effect. You may be pleasantly surprised.

Teenagers

Teenagers are growing so fast and have so many changes happening in their lives that they often require extra amounts of sleep. Getting up in the morning in time for school can offer a challenge and even a blaring alarm does not always arouse them. Try sitting next to them on their bed in the morning and give them a little Reiki. Soon you will notice their eyes begin to flutter as they slowly awake. What a nice way to start your day, showered with love.

Apply Reiki when their legs hurt from growing pains or when they are concerned about a test they need to take at school. Remember, Reiki works on not only the physical body but the mental body as well. Apply an intellectual balance on their chakras and see if it helps them recall the information they studied. Emotions run high at this age and the emotional balance can help when they are disturbed with an incident in school or with a friend. Show them how to apply these techniques themselves to ease them in troubled times when you are not around.

Animals

Animals are so receptive to the energy of Reiki you just may find your pets becoming Reiki junkies. Every time you administer a self Reiki treatment they show up in the room and soak in the energy. It is easy to give them a treatment for the mere act of petting an animal will begin the flow of Reiki. Then with conscious intent it becomes even stronger. There is no need to spend time studying their anatomy because Reiki will flow where it needs to go without our direction but if you're curious, know that an animal's chakras are in close proximity to the ones found in the human body.

When you begin a Reiki treatment on yourself or another they magically find their way to where you are and become part of the treatment. It may appear they are receiving the healing but indeed they are also bringing in their form of healing and support. Let them know you are aware of the gift they are bringing and they will become your healing assistance.

Example: I find my birds respond when I am giving treatments and they let me know when I am on track, in fact, some of my clients notice their response before I do. Communicating with animals is not as difficult as you might imagine. There is help all around us and with the gift of Reiki flowing in our bodies we can open to it and become more aware of these subtle messages.

Reiki goes where it is required in any body without the practitioner knowing or understanding where that might be. So with an animal, do not worry about hand positions. Hold the animal or direct the Reiki to them in a general fashion; Reiki will find its way to the place in the body where there is the most need. For the animal you cannot hold, position your hands in their direction and beam Reiki to them; it can even be sent through your eyes alone. Use this technique for pets that are not inclined to be held such as birds and fish.

In the case of wild animals direct the energy out to them. Even if they run away the energy will follow and assist them. Sometimes a bird will fly into a window and fall to the ground, injured and frightened. As you send Reiki out to them, the healing love will surround them and protect them from predators until they regain their strength. There is no wrong way to give Reiki to another; animal, human or vegetation all profit from its unconditional love.

Plants

When a plant is diseased, a continual direction of Reiki will abate the insects and give the plant a chance to recover. When you pass by the plant during the day or while giving it water, take just a moment to hold your hand out to it and

direct a little Reiki towards it. In the garden as you sow your seeds, beam Reiki into the ground and to the sky, asking for the proper amount of rain and sun for their growth. Plant your garden in the spring and take a moment to give each plant the attention of Reiki; you will be surprised how quickly they will grow. If you also plant according to the moon cycles you will see vast improvement in the yield of flowers, fruits and vegetables. This is true organic gardening.

Do not limit your use of the healing love of Reiki; if something has energy, and everything does, then give it Reiki. We can heal the planet, balance the stock market, calm the emotions of the people in a funeral procession driving by and send compassion to those in an ambulance. It only takes a moment to do and you may never know the assistance you have given another. Know you have the power to change the world, one incident at a time. Trust your divine gifts and power.

Practical Hands-on Healing

Because a massage table is not a common household item, here are some suggestions for a comfortable place for the client. Second best to using a massage table would be a foam pad on a strong table. Rectangular kitchen tables with thick strong legs work best and some dining room tables may work as well. The third selection would be a couch, with the client lying on the cushions and the practitioner sitting on a stool or a strong coffee table while they hold the hand positions. A bed would be the next best choice, depending on the type of bed. In conventional beds the client will need to lie closer to the center, then the practitioner will need to stretch to reach them, which can become a problem for an hour treatment. Newer beds have a firm outer core so that the client may lie close to the edge without feeling as if they will roll off. Using this type of bed will create less stress on the practitioners' back.

When giving energy healing to patients in hospitals, nurses have told me that sitting on the bed is permissible. The patient is usually positioned in the center of the bed and it can be difficult to reach them from the outside edge.

If the practitioner has an agile body, working on the floor with the client on a thick pad can also work. This technique is great on a warm summer day, on the grass, under the shade of a tree. When working outside, be sure to invite the energy of nature into the session.

When a horizontal position is not possible, having the receiver of the energy in a chair is apropos. Hold only the positions that can be easily reached. The cosmic energy is divinely guided and will be directed to the places that need the most healing, so hand positions are not as important as the intent to give healing energy. The lower positions on the body can bring a strain on the back and legs of the practitioner, so spend more time on the upper body and the energy will flow to the lower extremities as well. Remember Reiki is guided by the higher self and will transfer to the places that are not touched if needed without the direction of the practitioner.

Once you acquire the ability to transfer energy, the possibilities are endless. The best way to increase and discover your powers is to trade out treatments with other practitioners. Three or more participants are best, for you will have someone to compare notes with while picking up information while scanning the body and sending energy into it. Do not make it a solemn occasion. There is no need to be totally quiet, so discuss what you are feeling and sensing. Ask the other practitioners what they feel; this supports the individual process of each participant. There is no wrong way to share this pure love which is flowing through your head, heart and hands. You cannot do it wrong and you cannot hurt anyone with it, so just let it flow, and for Pete's sake, have fun.

Preparation of the Space before a Healing Treatment

1. Light a candle.
2. Connect heart to heart with your client and listen for guidance.
3. Play soft music.
4. Be creative. Give a treatment outside, under a big tree.
5. Use crystals or stones to aid in your healing ability.
6. Aromatherapy mixes well with the holistic energy work of Reiki.

Exchanging Reiki with other practitioners:
1. Exchange names and addresses with other students in your class.
2. By doing Reiki on each other, you will build confidence in your Reiki skills.
3. To build your clientele you may exchange with body workers other than Reiki students.
   a. Massage therapists
   b. Chiropractors
   c. Estheticians
   d. Acupuncturists

The benefits of doing Reiki on yourself every day.
1. Keeps your channel open and clear.
2. Helps to intensify your intuitive side.
3. Allows your emotional blocks to come up and to be handled and identified easily.
4. Balances your emotions and creates mental clarity.

Reiki Energy is universal energy, the power that connects us to all life. It is pure love.
1. We are a channel of this light, but the clarity of the vessel will determine its power.
2. Maintaining harmony and balance in life increases our power.

3. When Reiki is used on either the self or another, it builds and makes the practitioner's body a clearer vessel through which the healing energy flows.

The fee for Reiki treatments is usually about equal to the fee for massage treatments in your area. A new practitioner may doubt their abilities at first, but this is channeled energy; it is beyond the limitations of the self. Therefore, when determining your Reiki fees do not sell yourself short. If you think you are worth it, so will others and of course that also works in reverse. Words have power. Listen to how you describe yourself and your abilities. Keep it positive even if you don't believe it. Someday, very soon, you will.

Legislation varies from place to place, but at this time there are very few cities in the United States that require a license for Reiki. The body is not manipulated with hands-on healing; therefore, the client cannot be harmed by the unskilled. Regulations have been presented from time to time by those hoping to control metaphysical treatments, but nothing to date has been passed. It is wise to check the current laws for the area where you intend to practice to reassure this rule is still true.

Some practitioners feel more comfortable if the client signs a release form. In the Light Internal system of healing we are focused on a more positive approach. Energetically there is no fear about who shows up and how they may be in conflict after a treatment; therefore, no release forms are presented. Nevertheless, there are forms included in this book for those who may feel the need. Progress and treatment forms are used to keep track of what transpired in current and previous sessions; this will assist in future appointments.

Aura Energy Boost

This action will provide a quick pick-me-up and is a fun way to show off your newfound Reiki skills. As your hands move past the chakras, you will be clearing

and opening all of the chakras. Next, you will lift off the tired energy as you direct your hands up through the chakras. Finally, as your hands pass back down through the chakras, your intent is to have the chakras close down to where they need to be for that day.

Your hands will not be directly on the body, the body is sandwiched in between the hands while you stand to the side of your client. Place your hands about three to six inches off the body as you work in the auric field. The fingers of the hands are together as they cup the energy in your hands. Reiki bounces back and forth between the hands with the body in-between receiving the energy. At the crown chakra, have your hands facing each other, about eight inches apart. Imagine lightning bolts transferring back and forth. Once this image is clear in the mind's eye, move your hands over the third eye at the forehead. The energy is still moving from one hand to the next but now the chakra is between the hands, receiving Reiki. This is what opens and clears the chakra. Pay attention to what you are feeling.

- Is there more energy in the front or the back of the body?
- Is there a sense of need in a particular chakra?
- Is the sensation cold or hot?

This is a practice in awareness. There is no need to decipher why there are differences. Just feel, take note, and mention what was felt to the client.

Continue down the chakras. When you reach the heart, stay in the center of the body at the heart chakra, not to the left where the physical heart resides. Notice how you feel as you channel Reiki into the body of another. When you give Reiki, you get Reiki. Notice any sensations in your field. The receiver may feel tingling in their hands or feel a bit unsteady on their feet. To stabilize their stance have the client stand with their feet hip width apart. The base chakra is done quickly because it can be hard on the knees of the practitioner to stoop and reach this chakra.

Once Reiki has been placed into each chakra, the palms of the hands of the practitioner are turned up as they move up to the top of the head. Notice if more weight is felt in the hands as the old, tired energy is lifted off. At the crown, touch the little fingers together while hands are facing up to close the circuit. Turn the hands face down and lower them back to the knees. The hands should be in the front and back of the client's body. Snap the fingers at the knees to break and release the connection from the client to practitioner.

Ask the client what they sensed and share where you felt differences as well. This makes the exercise tangible and brings a new awareness of the body to the client. As this process is done, your client may begin to sway from the intense energy flowing into their body. They may feel tingling in their hands, or they could experience the warmth and energy coming from your hands. This is a wonderful way to familiarize someone with Reiki because it is so quick.

 Life Tool: Aura Energy Boost

1.	Client is standing and you are positioned standing at their side.
2.	Hold each of the following positions for 30 seconds or more. Follow your inner knowing.
3.	Place your hands with palms facing each other, about eight inches apart and a few inches above the crown.
4.	Once you feel an energy connection you may move your hands to the third eye, one hand in front and one in back of head; not touching the body.
5.	Continue opening and clearing each chakra as you go down the body, with your hands in the front and back of the client's body.
6.	Throat chakra.
7.	Heart chakra.
8.	Solar Plexus, just above navel.

9. Spleen chakra, just below navel.
10. Root chakra, located at the base of the tailbone.
11. Turn palms up and slowly lift the energy as your hands ascend towards the crown, then touch little fingers together to close the circuit.
12. Turn palms down and lower hands along outside of the front and back of the body, stopping at the knees.
13. Snap your fingers to break the energy connection between you and the client.
14. Share any information received.

Meditation

It is helpful to take time during the day to still your mind. This allows intuitive thoughts to surface. Center yourself by sitting and paying attention to your body. Notice if your legs are "antsy," if there is stiffness in your back, where you are holding tension in this moment. Follow your thoughts. There is no need to judge or change them; just watch them. Imagine opening the chakra at the top of your head and allowing the cosmic light to flow. What do you perceive? Are there colors, images, a scent, a sound, or an inner knowing that something is happening? With practice, you will become more in touch with feeling channeled energy. Divine energy is always present, but in the midst of our busy lives, it is often ignored and often goes unnoticed. This practice will reawaken your inherent senses.

We have the ability to create what happens to us and around us. In fact, we do it all the time, but are not always aware of it. In the course of meditation, this skill is revised and honed until it becomes automatic. To claim the ability of our creative thoughts, we must become acquainted with the divine essence, which is in every living thing, including us.

The following exercise is designed to open the awareness of all that lies within. It is a quick "pick me up" which can be done in as little as ten minutes while sitting at work or in the car before one begins to drive home. See it as a mini vacation to relieve stress and claim what is rightfully yours. It is free, quick and it is everywhere. All you need do is contact the proper channel.

 Life Tool: Golden Light Transfer

1.	Relax and still your body by breathing slowly and deeply.
2.	Let go of your problems by imagining you can set them in a bag and then place them outside of your door.
3.	Breathe in the cool energy of harmony and love.
4.	Exhale frustrations and tension in the heat of your breath.
5.	Turn your thoughts towards a golden light and visualize it entering the top of your head, noticing the sensation it makes. If none is sensed just imagine a feeling.
6.	Let the light begin to fill your body, starting at your toes.
7.	As the light continues to flow in, it fills your feet and gradually moves into your entire body. As you fill up with light, feel each muscle relaxing.
8.	The calm feeling makes your muscles become heavy as you sense sinking a little deeper into the chair.
9.	In your mind's eye, travel to your favorite place.
10.	This could be on the beach, in a field or under a tree.
11.	Is it sunny? Warm or cool? Is the wind blowing?
12.	What scents do you smell? Are there flowers, green grass or perhaps an

ocean?
13. Completely immerse yourself in the calm feeling of being in this space.
14. In this quiet state, in a location designed by you, focus on the golden light which has entered your body.
15. This light holds your personal divine essence; give it a feeling if one does not arise.
16. Know in your heart that from this moment on, you have the ability to create and become all that you desire to be.

 Life Tool: Chakra Meditation

1.	Follow steps 1 through 7 of the Golden Light Transfer and continue with the following.
2.	Visualize the 1st chakra at the base of your spine as a luscious red color. Allow this chakra to open like a fragrant red rose.
3.	In your mind's eye, move up to the 2nd chakra, just below your navel.
	a. See this chakra as orange in color.
	b. It could be as colorful as a poppy, opening to the sunlight.
4.	Visualize placing your energy into the 3rd chakra, just above the navel.
	a. It is the color of the bright golden sun.
	b. Allow it to take the form of a sweet yellow daisy.
	c. Take a moment to enjoy its aroma.
5.	Lift your awareness into the center of your chest at the 4th chakra, your heart center.

a.	This center is green, so focus on soft green ferns.
b.	The sensation is warm, moist and comforting.

6. In the throat, visualize the 5th chakra opening, exposing a deep powerful color of blue.

    a. The color takes the form of a morning glory.

    b. At first tightly twisted and then gently unwinding as it opens to the warm rays of the sun.

7. Moving your attention up to your forehead, visualize the 6th chakra.

    a. See it as the dark blue-purple color of indigo.

    b. Imagine a tall, regal, iridescent iris.

    c. Enjoy its piquant aroma.

8. Over the top of your head, visualize the 7th chakra as a vibrant violet color.

    a. This chakra connects you to the clear essence of your inner light.

    b. This is where the cosmic power enters.

9. Continue to relax, floating through your chakras, entering the ones that call for your attention.

10. When you feel complete, draw your energy up from your base chakra through the entire chakra system, until your energy gently lifts out of your crown.

11. Take a deep breath, connect to the earth, open your eyes, and feel completely revived.

Chapter 6

The Forms

The forms in this chapter are designed to document the Reiki process for the student as well as the client. Also they give basic information to hand out to the client.

Recipient Information Form

The information contained within this form should be kept confidential and when it is time to dispose of this form it should be shredded to protect the privacy of the individual. There are times when contacting a client after a treatment is compassionate while other times it is best to let the client process the treatment in their own way and time. When obtaining email contacts know they can be used in marketing but permission should always be received before sending out mass emails and newsletters. When you present pertinent information in your mailings, clients will often respond affirmatively.

Progress and Treatment Report

Here you can keep a record of how often a client comes for a treatment, note if you used any "Life Tools" to help them be aware of the possible origin of their distress and what their reactions were during the treatment.

Chakra Cleansing Journal

After a Reiki attunement the 21-day cleanse will begin. Close observation of physical differences as well as emotional and mental attitudes will allow the student to understand and process faster. By keeping a small journal, common threads will begin to weave and new awareness about the self will float to the surface. The practice of writing down thoughts can be a valuable tool.

What is a Reiki Treatment?

When you offer Reiki to another, the gift will be better used and understood if the participant is aware of how Reiki can influence their body and thus their life. Copy this form and give it to your perspective client by email or present it before they come for their treatment. If they do not have the form prior to their treatment, remember to explain the Reiki process to them and the possible effects. Then give them this form to take home so they may continue to be observant to the physical, mental, emotional and spiritual changes in their life.

Client Information Form

I, the undersigned, understand the Reiki session is for the purpose of assisting in stress reduction and relaxation. I understand very clearly a Reiki session is not a substitute for medical or psychological diagnosis and treatment. Reiki practitioners do not diagnose conditions, nor do they prescribe or perform medical treatment, nor prescribe substances, nor interfere with the treatment of a licensed medical professional. It is recommended I see a licensed physician or other licensed health care professional for any physical or psychological ailment I have.

Signature: _____ Date: _____

Print Name: _____

Address: _____

City: _____ State: _____

Zip Code: _____ e-mail: _____

Phone – Home: _____ Work: _____ Cell: _____

Session Date	Remarks	Progress and Treatment

Progress and Treatment Report

Date	Remarks	Progress and Treatment

What is a Reiki Treatment?

1. Reiki works on our four bodies.
   a. Physical: the body and pain.
   b. Mental: thoughts running in the mind.
   c. Emotional: what is felt?
   d. Spiritual: the love held for self and others.

2. Reiki works on the original cause of the dis-ease.
   a. New perceptions of the cause of discomfort are realized.
   b. Because of the accelerated effect of Reiki, one may feel "off" or unbalanced for a short time. This is the process of the bodies clearing.

3. How a treatment is performed:
   a. The recipient lies on a table with shoes removed.
   b. The practitioner lightly touches the body starting at the head and continuing down the body.
   c. The recipient may be asked to turn over for treatment on the back.
   d. Falling asleep is a way a recipient might choose to still the mind, thus allowing for a deeper healing to take place. The Reiki is still working, even during sleep.
   e. The recipient will feel relaxing energy that will allow them to release their thoughts and enjoy the treatment.
   f. Treatments can also be done while the recipient is sitting in a chair, or at a distance when the recipient is unable to be physically present.

4. Reiki will continue to work for three days after the treatment. Therefore, for chronic problems, repeat the sessions every 3 or 4 days for at least 3 consecutive treatments.
   a. The treatment will initially relax the body; after this calmness subsides, the energy will still be felt either mentally, emotionally, spiritually or any combination of these.

b. A mental clearing stills the mind (allowing one to sleep) or Reiki can bring in a feeling of being unfocused.

c. Emotional release may bring up tears, which may be unexplainable.

d. A spiritual healing may bring in a feeling for the love of nature, a feeling of gratitude or peaceful thoughts.

e. All of these feelings will subside at the end of three days as new perceptions are realized.

f. Watch how you perceive old negative situations. Are you less attached to the outcome?

g. Watch for an increase of coincidences or strange synchronicities.

h. Reiki works 100% of the time. Notice where the healing is occurring: physically, mentally, emotionally and/or spiritually.

~ Reiki is pure love ~

Using the journal will keep the student aware of their rising vibration in each of the four bodies and all seven chakras. It will assist to ground the incoming light and to keep one in the present time. Keep the memoranda short to encourage and support the process each day.

Day 1   Chakra 1

_____
_____
_____
_____
_____
_____

Day 2   Chakra 2

_____
_____
_____
_____
_____
_____

Day 3   Chakra 3

_____
_____
_____
_____
_____
_____
_____

Day 4   Chakra 4

_____
_____
_____
_____
_____
_____

Day 5   Chakra 5

_____
_____
_____
_____
_____
_____

Day 6   Chakra 6

_____
_____
_____
_____
_____
_____

Day 7   Chakra 7

_____
_____
_____
_____
_____
_____

Day   8   Chakra 1

_____
_____
_____
_____
_____
_____
_____

Day   9   Chakra 2

_____
_____
_____
_____
_____
_____

Day   10   Chakra 3

_____
_____
_____
_____
_____
_____

Day   11   Chakra 4

_____
_____
_____
_____
_____
_____

Day   12   Chakra 5

_____
_____
_____
_____
_____
_____
_____
_____

Day   13   Chakra 6
_____
_____
_____
_____
_____
_____

Day   14   Chakra 7
_____
_____
_____
_____
_____
_____

Day 15   Chakra 1
_____
_____
_____
_____
_____
_____
_____

Day   16   Chakra 2

_____
_____
_____
_____
_____
_____

Day   17   Chakra 3

_____
_____
_____
_____

Day   18   Chakra 4

_____
_____
_____
_____
_____
_____

Day   19   Chakra 5

_____
_____
_____
_____
_____
_____
_____

Day 20 Chakra 6

_____

_____

_____

_____

_____

_____

Day 21 Chakra 7

_____

_____

_____

_____

_____

_____

Afterword

Though healing abilities can be taught and transferred, innate curative capabilities must be found within your own being and world and claimed as your own. Reiki holds a key but it is you who needs to find the door which aligns with your path. Reiki opens the awareness to perceive your gifts and sustains you as a leader, not a follower.

Marnie's coaching and lectures make use of many energy systems which help heal the body and spirit of negative experiences of the past. This allows people to cut the destructive mental and emotional bonds attached to them and experience a creative, powerful and personal freedom they never knew they had.

The ideas and concepts in this book will allow you to transform your life rather quickly. It is a guide to enlighten and assist you to your highest potential in a way that is simple. This transformation does not have to be complex. Life is meant to be and can be a joy. That is not to say that it will not have its challenges, which is what gives life variety and interest. So I invite you to enter with me on this journey of the soul, to walk with a light step as you become the observer of your own path.

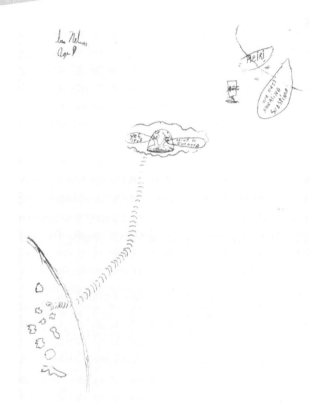

This picture shows how a young boy perceives the Reiki energy. Ian was only 9 years old when he created this drawing. His space men are asking for a "healing substance." The others respond by saying "Reiki is our need, yes it is."

Even small children can sense the need of Reiki healing love for our planet. Do not over estimate the power of these little beings and their desire to help. Share your knowledge with the children and they will no doubt respond with surprising awareness.

Notes

Notes

Notes

Appendix

The following is a collection of books to increase your understanding of Reiki, chakras and the exoteric thus allowing you to know yourself better.

Empowerment Through Reiki by Paula Horan. Best book to start learning about Reiki. No hand positions, just basic information on Reiki, not too metaphysical.

The Complete Book of Chakra Healing by Cyndi Dale. Here you will find a good description of the chakras, written so that even the novice can understand. It includes many exercises to help understand your energy and how it relates to your chakras.

Heal Your Body by Louise Hay. Inexpensive book on ailments and emotions, gives lists of physical problems, emotions connected to them, and affirmations.

Feelings Buried Alive Never Die by Karol K. Truman. A more extensive book on emotions and the body, lots of references to other books to back up information, a more extensive list of ailments in the back.

Essential Reiki by Diane Stein. Presents a good overall view of Reiki with information on all levels of Reiki.

Anatomy of the Spirit by Carolyn Myss. Explains how there is a common thread that runs through many spiritual practices. It connects the chakras to the Seven Sacraments of the Catholic religion and the Kabbalah written in the Jewish religion.

Energy Anatomy by Carolyn Myss. A tape series which explains the chakras in a way that even the novice can understand.

Hands of Light by Barbara Brennan. A healer's Bible; it takes years to get through the information in this book. The writer is very left brain-oriented, so it's very detailed—and worth the time to understand. Many exercises on working with chakras and auras.

Power of Reiki by Tanmaya Honervogt. Beautiful color pictures on every page, visually expressing how Reiki works.

Bodymind Workbook by Debbie Shapiro. Gives a clear understanding on how the body and mind work together, giving signals to open emotional issues. There is also shown a connection of the bones, tissues and fluids in the body and how they, too, give clues to how our emotions are reacting in our body.

Bibliography

Dale, Cyndy *The Complete Book of Chakra Healing*. St. Paul MI: Llewellyn, 2009.

Grey, Alex. *Sacred Mirrors*. Rochester VT: Inner Traditions International,1990.

Hay, Louise. *Heal Your Body*. Carson, CA: Hay House, Inc., 1982

Mitchell , Karyn. *Reiki: A Torch in Daylight*. St. Charles, IL: Mind Rivers Publishing, 1994.

Myss, Caroline. *Anatomy of the Spirit: the Seven Stages of Power and Healing*. New York City, NY: Harmony Books, 1997.

Petter , Frank Arjava *Reiki Fire*. Netherlands: Motilal Banarsidass Publishers Private Limited,1997.

Rand, William Lee. *Reiki: The Healing Touch*. Southfield, Mi.: Vision Publications, 1998.

Tansley, David. *Radionics and the Subtle Bodies of Man*. Essex: Saffron Walden, 1972.

Truman, Karol. *Feelings Buried Alive Never Die*. St. George, UT: Olympus Distributing, 1991.

Index

2

21-day cleanse...50

A

abuser..17
addictions 35, 92
affirmations 59, 103, 104, 145
alexandrite..92
amazonite..92
amber 90, 91, 92
amethyst..92
angels...18, 62
animal 15, 41
anxiety 18
aquamarine 91, 92
arthritis 14, 15, 27
*attunement*12, 13, 15, 18, 21, 32, 44, 46, 47, 48, 50, 72, 99, 129
aura.................56, 77, 97, 98, 101, 102, 106
aventurine 90
awareness. 13, 17, 33, 35, 49, 122, 124, 129, 141
azurite...92

B

balance 21, 28, 54, 55, 59, 91, 103, 120
Beaming...101, 102
beggar...27
belief..14, 15, 97
benefit 15, 76
Bible...24, 146
black tourmaline...................................90
blessing...19, 33, 77
bloodstone 91

body 11, 12, 13, 14, 16, 17, 18, 19, 20, 21, 25, 27, 32, 35, 39, 40, 41, 43, 44, 47, 48, 49, 50, 52, 54, 55, 59, 60, 61, 65, 70, 76, 77, 79, 81, 82, 83, 84, 86, 90, 93, 94, 95, 96, 97, 98, 99, 100, 101, 102, 103, 104, 105, 106, 107, 109, 111, 120, 121, 122, 124, 129, 132, 145, 146
Buddha...24, 93

C

car 78, 124
Chakra Cleansing Journal...............129, 134
chakra(s) ...11, 35, 36, 37, 44, 50, 51, 54, 55, 56, 61, 75, 77, 81, 83, 84, 90, 91, 92, 106, 121, 122, 124
channeling............15, 30, 39, 46, 82, 97, 101
child 2, 45, 46, 83, 84
children 2, 3, 4, 15, 46, 141
Christian.....................................12, 24, 29
circle..25, 27, 73
citrine..90, 91, 92
clairvoyance 92
cleanse 35, 48, 49, 50, 51, 107, 129
client ... 19, 39, 40, 41, 52, 54, 71, 72, 76, 86, 93, 94, 95, 96, 97, 99, 100, 101, 102, 103, 104, 105, 106, 107, 119, 120, 121, 122, 128, 129
colors 13, 44, 49
compassion 17, 91, 93
concentration 92
consciousness 11, 19, 26, 32, 47, 90, 101
coral 90
cords 35, 107
creativity 54, 90, 92
crown chakra 11, 44, 47, 48, 95, 96, 121

D

Degree ....iii, 35, 36
diamond...92
dis-ease 16, 17, 82, 86, 97, 101, 132
diseased ....*See* dis-ease
distress.........................17, 18, 43, 86, 129
divine intelligence.............................. 18, 48
dream.. 92, 95
dyslexia 55, 59, 104

E

emerald.. 91
emotional balance 54
emotional body.....13, 16, 17, 18, 20, 21, 22,
   28, 35, 40, 43, 48, 51, 70, 82, 83, 86, 94,
   96, 97, 103, 107, 120, 129, 146
emotions.13, 16, 17, 21, 40, 50, 94, 96, 145,
   146
energy.11, 12, 13, 14, 15, 17, 18, 19, 20, 21,
   24, 26, 27, 28, 32, 35, 36, 39, 40, 41, 43,
   44, 46, 47, 48, 49, 50, 51, 52, 53, 54, 55,
   59, 61, 70, 71, 72, 73, 75, 76, 77, 78, 81,
   82, 83, 90, 92, 93, 94, 95, 96, 97, 98, 99,
   100, 101, 102, 103, 105, 106, 107,
   119,☰120, 121, 122, 124, 132, 141, 145
energy blocks 21, 106
etheric. 12, 13, 24, 40, 48, 50, 54, 70, 81, 82,
   101
ethics.. 90, 92

F

faith... 92
flow11, 12, 14, 16, 18, 27, 39, 40, 41, 43, 44,
   47, 50, 51, 56, 70, 71, 73, 76, 82, 94, 99,
   102, 104, 124
fluorite 91
food.. 26, 78, 79, 90
forgiveness... 17, 91

G

gold 26, 90, 91, 92
grounding 56, 90, 103, 106
guides........... 21, 36, 43, 59, 62, 71, 72, 100
guilt 90

H

hand positions..35
hands...12, 13, 14, 15, 17, 18, 19, 24, 27, 28,
   35, 39, 40, 42, 44, 46, 52, 54, 55, 56, 59,
   61, 71, 78, 86, 95, 97, 99, 101, 102, 103,
   104, 105, 106, 107, 120, 121, 122
harm...15
Hawaii 30
Hayashi 30, 32, 34
headaches 83, 84
heal 13, 16, 17, 18, 24, 25, 26, 27, 35, 47, 62
healer 18, 19, 28, 71, 72, 99, 101, 146
healing.11, 12, 14, 15, 17, 18, 19, 21, 24, 25,
   27, 28, 29, 30, 33, 35, 36, 39, 40, 41, 43,
   44, 46, 47, 51, 52, 53, 54, 59, 61, 70, 71,
   76, 82, 86, 93, 94, 95, 99, 101, 102, 103,
   106, 107, 119, 120, 121, 132, 133, 140,
   141
healing power (s).............................. 12, 33
healthy ....59, 63, 82, 104, 109, *See* health
heart....11, 12, 16, 17, 18, 29, 35, 39, 40, 44,
   46, 52, 54, 55, 56, 60, 61, 64, 91, 94, 103,
   104, 110, 119, 122
heart chakra 11, 122
honor....15, 22, 28, 31, 33, 39, 44, 72, 90, 91

I

illness 16, 19, 44
initiate 18, 20, 44, 46, 47, 48, 50
intellectual balance 54, 103
intent...14, 41, 52, 59, 71, 75, 76, 83, 93, 94,
   95, 102, 103, 121
intuition......... 17, 26, 30, 43, 48, 51, 99, 100
intuitive 14, 35, 39, 46, 94, 95, 120, 124

J

Jesus 24, 25, 93

K

knowledge .... v, 24, 25, 40, 50, 55, 141
kyanite 92

L

lapis 92
laying on of hands 24
levels 28, 30, 34, 36, 47, 93, 95, 145
Life Tool 86
light11, 12, 16, 17, 18, 26, 28, 29, 36, 39, 41, 54, 56, 69, 72, 74, 76, 77, 78, 81, 82, 86, 94, 95, 97, 102, 103, 106, 120, 124, 134
lineage 31, 32, 33
listen 16, 48, 53, 119
love ..v, 11, 12, 13, 15, 16, 17, 18, 19, 20, 21, 28, 39, 40, 44, 49, 52, 56, 60, 61, 62, 65, 72, 77, 83, 84, 86, 90, 91, 93, 94, 101, 105, 111, 120, 132, 133, 141

M

malachite 91
martial arts, ... 30
master 13, 30, 31, 32, 34, 36, 44, 93
medication....................................14, 15, 16
meditation ... 18, 27, 32, 50, 51, 78, 124, 152
memories.................................... 18
mental body ... 13, 16, 17, 18, 20, 35, 40, 48, 54, 70, 83, 94, 96, 97, 107, 129, 133
message...............................48, 94
mind.... 17, 50, 69, 70, 71, 72, 75, 76, 83, 94, 95, 121, 124, 132, 133, 146
moldavite.................................... 92
monastery..............................24, 25, 26, 27
Mother Earth 32, 56, 61, 77, 103, 106
movie.. 70

O

oneness...............................16, 19, 54, 82, 93
over-the-counter drugs............................ 19

P

pain12, 13, 14, 15, 17, 20, 26, 27, 28, 42, 83, 86, 132
passion.. 90
pendulum.................................... 35
perception 92
peridot 90, 91
perspective 13, 17, 83, 129
plant.. 15
power ... vi, 12, 22, 30, 31, 33, 46, 59, 61, 62, 69, 71, 73, 74, 76, 77, 78, 79, 90, 91, 92, 93, 97, 101, 102, 103, 106, 107, 120, 141
practitioner16, 18, 19, 32, 35, 39, 40, 41, 44, 47, 52, 55, 71, 72, 76, 86, 94, 95, 99, 101, 102, 120, 122, 132
prayer.. 25, 52, 71
Progress and Treatment Report 96, 129
protection 20, 39, 61, 77, 83, 92
pyrite....................................... 90, 91

Q

QuanYin 93
quartz... 90, 91, 92

R

Radionics.................................... 71, 82, 147
receive 22, 26, 33, 51, 54, 59, 69, 70, 81, 82, 95, 103, 106, 107
Recipient Information Form 128, 130
red garnet 90, 91
red jasper 90
released 21, 48, 71, 86, 104, 107, 109
religious 11, 14, 15, 71
rhodochrosite 90, 91
ruby... 90

S

sapphire 92
Scanning... 99, 101
selenite 92
silver cord 61, 106, 107
smoky quartz 90, 91
spiritual body ..12, 13, 16, 18, 19, 21, 30, 40,
    43, 46, 47, 48, 70, 83, 92, 93, 95, 96, 97,
    107, 133, 145, 152
star 26, 30, 70
sugilite.. 92
symbols 26, 30, 31, 32, 35, 36, 69, 70, 71, 78

T

Takata 29, 30, 31, 32, 33, 34
Teenagers 115
the gift 22, 25, 28, 31, 32, 33, 44, 129
thoughts
    thought.....17, 20, 92, 102, 124, 129, 132,
    133
tiger eye 90, 91
topaz 90, 92
touch......15, 24, 39, 43, 47, 52, 86, 122, 124
tourmaline 91, 92
traditional 19, 31, 32, 33, 34, 36, 97
traffic 15
transcendent............................... 12, 18, 51

d

trauma..83, 99
treatment..15, 17, 18, 21, 35, 52, 55, 59, 76,
    78, 93, 94, 95, 96, 97, 102, 119, 121, 128,
    129, 130, 132
truth 29, 39, 60, 63, 83, 104, 110
turquoise...92

U

universal life force....................................12
universe.....11, 16, 18, 20, 27, 28, 39, 44, 71,
    74, 107
Usui 24, 25, 26, 27, 28, 29, 30, 31, 32, 34

V

vibration........ 13, 20, 32, 47, 48, 70, 71, 134
violet light 11, 75
vision questing 25
voice....................................... 39, 43, 48, 53

W

walk 18, 19, 27, 42, 94
water 49, 78, 79, 90, 94, 96, 107
What is a Reiki Treatment....... 107, 129, 132
wisdom..30
wrong 15, 27

Z

zircon...92

About the Author

Marnie Vincolisi has been lecturing on Reiki, metaphysics and spiritual growth for decades. Some of the classes she has developed are on subjects as varied as divination, space clearing, ear coning, sacred geometry, meditation and ascended masters. Marnie currently lives in the Southwestern United States; she travels throughout the country to lecture and gives attunements and treatments remotely. Her sessions are for optimal health, emotional balance, mental clarity and spiritual connection.

Marnie's meditation CDs and MP3s and other books may be found at
www.lightinternal.com
You may contact Marnie for personal sessions at
marnie@lightinternal.com

Programs by Marnie Vincolisi

Presentation slides to support the study of Reiki graphically illustrate the methods presented in this and other books by Marnie Vincolisi. The slides are suitable for class presentations and are available at www.lightinternal.com

Finding Your Inner Gift, the Ultimate Reiki 1ˢᵗ Degree Manual
Inner Gifts Uncovered, the Complete Reiki 2ⁿᵈ Degree Manual
Claiming Your Inner Gifts, the Comprehensive Study of Master Reiki

Meditation Made Easy and *Cosmic Connections* feature the melodic voice of Marnie Vincolisi in CD format. The CDs may be used for understanding our chakra systems through guided imagery meditation and for meditations during the attunement process for Reiki Master Teachers. Also found on *Meditation Made Easy* is the process for a Reiki self treatment, easily guided by Marnie, each available as a CD or an MP3 online at www.lightinternal.com

CPSIA information can be obtained at www.ICGtesting.com
Printed in the USA
BVOW101941140713

325909BV00005B/8/P